MINISTRY ENDORSEMENTS

In this hour, we need watchmen on the walls of our countries who can peer into the future, pray and respond. As we know, history belongs to the intercessors! In order to see, we need light provided by such leaders as Jon and Jolene Hamill. They are aptly called to be Lamplighters, revolutionaries who illuminate what, when and how to pray..."

Cindy Jacobs
Co-Founder, Generals International
Dallas, TX

The Body of Christ has many great teachers and writers, but few have been required to embody their message like Jon & Jolene Hamill. They teach us, not just from what they've learned, but from what they've lived. These guys get it...because they do it! Read this book!

Dutch Sheets
Founder, Dutch Sheets Ministries
Colorado Springs, CO

i

My friend Jon Hamill is one of the prophetic voices in this generation sounding a call to "governmental intercession." But this is not just theory with Jon. He has a wealth of experiences and testimonies of breakthroughs and transformations in cities and regions through this type of prayer.

Rick Ridings
Founder and Apostolic Overseer
Succat Hallel (24/7 worship and prayer overlooking the Temple Mount)
Jerusalem, Israel

....

Because of our location in Metro Washington, DC I've had the honor of hosting many well known men and women of God. I can honestly say that Jon and Jolene Hamill of Lamplighter Ministries are in a class by themselves. They listen to the heartbeat of God and share a living word for those they minister to. They have helped me build our local church and they can help you. I give Jon and Jolene my highest endorsement. They will always be welcome to minister anywhere that I have any influence.

H. Pitts Evans
Pastor, Whole Word Fellowship
Oakton VA

....

Jon and Jolene Hamill and Lamplighter Ministries are a shining light calling forth societal change while contending for a global awakening of unprecedented magnitude thru the prevailing power of prayer. It has been my honor and joy in this life to partner with the Hamills over the past several years. As a father in the global prayer and prophetic community, it is great delight to commend to you the passion for Jesus, the abundance of the fruit and gifts of the Holy Spirit and a walk of integrity that Jon and Jolene exhibit.

James W. Goll
Founder, God Encounters Ministries
Director Emeritus, Prayer Storm
Nashville, TN

....

Jon has a prophetic ability to see and interpret the unfolding spiritual reality behind the actions of men, historical and present day events. They look at the impact of men and women who are passionate for God, and willing to sacrifice life, wealth and sacred honor for the integrity of their faith and freedom. Nations have changed by their legacy. And we are compelled to change the course of history as well!

Dr. Martin Frankena
Rushing Streams Ministries
Reisterstown, MD

....

Jon and Jolene are genuine vibrant lovers of God. They are leading pilgrims to the freedom, strength and revelation of the Lord's current purposes and pursuits. I highly recommend them to the church as prophetic forerunners who bring God into a fuller view. They are uncommon vessels proclaiming prophetic insight to hearts crying out for more. I am honored to give this endorsement.

Jay Francis
Pastor, Rock Road Chapel, Berne NY

ABOUT CROWN & THRONE

Crown and Throne will revolutionize your prayer life and shift your paradigm into a prophetic dimension as you learn to address land issues, understand covenant, and advance in Kingdom authority in the earth realm.

I have great respect for Jon and his ministry and the honesty and simplicity that he expresses in his call to this land. This book, though directed toward America, can be used as a model for any nation. This is a day to overthrow thrones of iniquity. *Crown and Throne* takes the greatest model of our Messiah's triumph and invokes a people today to arise with the same selfless approach to seeing the glory overtake the earth. Read! Buy for others to read!

Chuck D. Pierce
President, Global Spheres Inc. and Glory of Zion International
Corinth, TX

THE MIDNIGHT CRY

Prophetic Perceptions for 2018 and beyond
including Donald Trump and national turnaround

JON & JOLENE HAMILL

BURNING LAMP™
—— media & publishing ——

THE MIDNIGHT CRY by Jon & Jolene Hamill

Published by BURNING LAMP MEDIA & PUBLISHING
www.burninglampmap.com | www.jonandjolene.us

Find us on Facebook and Twitter.
www.facebook.com/burninglampmap
@burninglampmap

Paperback
ISBN-10: 198146056X
ISBN-13: 978-198146-05-64

E-Book
ISBN-10: 198146056X
ISBN-13: 978-198146-05-64

Jon & Jolene Hamill
Lamplighter Ministries
www.lamplighterministries.net | jonandjolene.us

Cover Design by James Nesbit
www.jamesart.net

Printed in the United States of America
First Edition 2017

DEDICATION

It is with the utmost respect and gratitude that Jolene and I dedicate our second book "The Midnight Cry" to our incredible Lamplighter family. We have taken quite a journey together. And because of you, the world will never be the same.

No King but Jesus,

Jon & Jolene Hamill
Thanksgiving 2017

CONTENTS

INTRODUCTION
Your Midnight Summons

Reformation Day 2017, Washington DC. To Christians, October 31, 2017 marks the 500th anniversary of a spiritual revolution which forever changed the course of the western world—the Protestant Reformation. What a day to launch into a book project conveying "real-time" revelation to the body of Christ on "The Midnight Cry."

Because in this hour a reformation movement of God's Spirit is again beginning to sweep the earth. The "Midnight Cry" is a summons for this spiritual revolution.

But it is first a love story, between Jesus and His covenant people. It lays key pathways for you to become a catalyst for Christ's love and freedom in the nations. In many ways the book is a companion volume to our first book "Crown & Throne," documenting tangible results birthed from the principles within its pages. Both books are written to equip you as a spiritual revolutionary for this hour.

A few chapters of the "Midnight Cry" chronicle the historic turnaround in the 2106 elections which ushered Donald Trump into the presidency. We share our own prophetic words featuring President Trump from the very beginning. We also chronicle a few of the reformational policy turnarounds which have already defined his presidency.

Most importantly, we document the restoration of our covenantal foundations which served to catalyze this dramatic shift. No politician owns the turnaround. God does. And to a large extent, so do the intercessors who in the midnight hours prayed this nation through to the dawning of a new day.

That said, the "The Midnight Cry" is not first focused on politics or conflicts of thrones or governmental prayer. The primary focus is a "burning lamp awakening," a love relationship which awakens you and ignites your lamp of devotion to the Lord. God's glory is being restored on a global level as His new move is released. You can take your place among the forerunners who are right now preparing the way for this move.

As I look out over Washington DC—at the Capitol, the Supreme Court, the White House, the Lincoln Memorial—I realize the freedom symbolized by our nation's seats of authority may not have even existed had the Reformation not occurred. The reverberations of God's seismic shift not only ushered the western world into freedom of religion, but freedom of thought, freedom of speech, freedom of the press, freedom of governance, etc.

Perhaps the greatest revolution catalyzed by Martin Luther was not to counter the corruption of the church, or even to empower the common man. It was to re-focus the eyes of the western world away from idols, saints and substitute redeemers and back on to the Messiah of the world, Jesus Christ.

The hard road forward eventually even secured "liberty and justice for all," at least as an ideal, thanks in large part to a black preacher named after the famed reformer. His legacy revolutionized American life from the 20th century forward.

I'm talking, of course, about Martin Luther King.

King's revolutionary messages became a midnight cry that awakened

America and shifted us into new season of history. Echoing the cries of forerunners and revolutionaries through the ages, from Moses to David to John the Baptist to the Apostles and the Pilgrims, Wesley and Finney and Seymour and countless others known and unknown, who accomplished similar feats. They all brought a spiritual revolution to the wilderness of their world. The earth shook and shifted as a result.

America's revolution was ignited by a midnight cry from a patriot named Paul Revere. This midnight rider awakened America to fight for freedom. And in the governance of nations a new precedent was set.

Friends, we are in a reformational season of similar magnitude. It's time for your midnight cry to resound. To Heaven first, and then to awaken your world.

And it's time for you to ride.

Jesus Himself prophesied that the most revolutionary season in all of human history would be clearly marked by a midnight cry. Ushering a global "Moses movement" to counter a global "Pharaoh movement." You can feel the reverberations even now. My prayer is that the cry itself will open your eyes. And that your response will again change the world.

That said, never forget that the midnight cry is first a summons to a wedding. Behold the Bridegroom. He's coming. Rise up to meet Him!

Jon & Jolene Hamill
Lamplighter Ministries
Arlington VA

CHAPTER ONE

The Midnight Cry

prophetic perceptions 2018-2020

"Behold the Bridegroom. He's coming. Rise up to meet Him!" The most anticipated words in human history are described by Jesus as a "midnight cry". They signal His imminent return. In a pattern conveyed by ancient Hebrew customs, a Jewish Messiah is coming for His bride. Messengers will be sent before His face to announce His arrival. Across the nations, this bride is going to awaken, light her lamp, and join His great procession.

Recently the Lord began to highlight "the midnight cry" to me as a prophetic message to describe His work in 2018 through 2020 and beyond. I was at first surprised. Many who read Jesus' parable of the wise and foolish virgins believe it refers solely to the end times. After all, it clearly prophesies the return of the Bridegroom—in a midnight hour of history known as the end of days.

Are we really that far down the road right now?

Not yet. But as you will see, Matthew 25, the passage surrounding this "midnight cry," actually projects not only into the end of days but into every season of renewal and spiritual revolution that God initiates. They are all rooted in these amazing words.

And we are in one of these very seasons right now. Corresponding with the 500th anniversary of the Protestant Reformation and the 70th anniversary of the rebirth of Israel, a long-prophesied move of awakening has begun. History will soon bear witness that it is of a similar magnitude to these epoch-defining events. Incorporated into God's move in America is a dramatic, midnight turnaround from idolatry-empowered globalism which impacted the 2016 elections and ushered Donald Trump into power. This power shift has unleashed dramatic reverberations not only throughout America, but Israel and the nations as well. We'll explore this in depth later in the book.

That said, no political figure owns the turnaround. God does. And it's part of a much larger movement now being birthed by the Spirit of the Lord. The Midnight Cry has been written to provide you with depth and breadth to see the potential of this move, and enter into its fullness.

Behold the Bridegroom. He's coming. Rise up to meet Him!

Ten Keys for 2018 and Beyond

Here are ten keys to the "midnight cry" of Matthew 25 which are full of prophetic significance for 2018-2020. We're going to explore many of them more thoroughly later. The parable conveys:

1. *A midnight crisis*—It's really dark out there. We haven't fully understood the magnitude of what we've been confronting. Then suddenly breakthrough comes and there's no more delay. Both challenges and answers to many prayers will be coming suddenly this season.

2. *A midnight watch*—We must keep a midnight watch to shift the midnight crisis. Signals in the night will become a new standard for revelation these next few years.

3. *A midnight turnaround*—We will continue to receive breakthrough in the spirit of a magnitude which can only come as a verdict from Heaven's court. Remember Jesus judges and makes war to enforce His judgements in the earth realm. We will perceive this very clearly these next few years.

4. *A midnight cry*—the midnight rider received and conveyed divine intelligence which positioned God's people to advance. There's a lot of rhetoric out there. But there's also a genuine cry resounding from many prophets who are accurately perceiving the movements of His Spirit in the earth. We must know His timing. Now a summons to a wedding is being sounded. Time to behold the Bridegroom once again!

5. *A midnight awakening*—the response to the midnight cry literally startles the bride awake. "Startling" is a key word for 2018. Many will be startled by God's work this year. Many who awoke in 2016, who went back to sleep in 2017, will be startled awake before 2020.

6. *Burning lamps lit*—as we awaken to Jesus in 2018, our lamps of devotion must be relit with fresh fire. Where you've been scattered, let your eyes again become focused so your body can be full of light. His glory is being restored! Watch for a "burning lamp movement" to arise. From region to region, God is resetting our lampstands and relighting the flame! And please remember that burning lamps bring exposure.

7. *The wise take oil*—the wise virgins are commended for investing now to secure their provision for the future. In this season of economic resurgence it is wise for you to do the same. Gain the oil of the Spirit and resources in the natural to succeed in the journey ahead.

8. *Exiting and entering*—Jesus is drawing His true disciples to Himself. Note that the bride leaves the door of her home to join the wedding procession, and then enters into the door of His celebration. We are now in a season of open doors. Therefore how you exit and enter becomes very important. Redeem the time. Get moving!

9. *New tabernacles movement*—always remember that the bridal

procession culminates under a bridal canopy. Look for a refreshing new season of intimacy to spring forth as God launches the next phase of His Amos 9:11 restoration of the Tabernacle of David. His glory will be a bridal canopy for His people!

10. *From Rome to Jerusalem*—This is part of the bridal procession this year as His menorah is being restored. God is emphasizing Hanukkah and Tabernacles for 2018. Watch how the lamp even becomes reunited with the tabernacle from 2018-2019. This will heal the eyes of the bride and fill her with 2020 vision.

End-Time, Real-Time

For many reasons, I personally believe we are in the beginning of the end-times drama prophesied by Jesus and the prophets. First and foremost because the greatest biblical demarcation has already occurred. In 1948 the nation of Israel was literally born again! This year marks the 70th anniversary of this miracle. Watch how God emphasizes "70" in this season. Lets also watch over Israel and the Temple Mount as the conflict of thrones continues.

THE MIDNIGHT RIDER RECEIVED AND CONVEYED REAL-TIME DIVINE INTELLIGENCE. LIKEWISE AS A COVENANT PEOPLE, WE MUST BECOME ALIGNED WITH HIS "NOW" TIMING.

A second reason is much more personal and subjective. When I first met prophet Bob Jones, he told me that he had seen me in a dream where he was shown many leaders who would serve in the end times. Probably not a big enough deal to persuade you. But it's a really big deal to me.

We could also look at the rise of globalism tied to idolatry, new biotechnology which fulfills ancient prophecy, artificial intelligence etc. But here's a final reason which I consider extremely viable. Perhaps the first time in church history the bride of Christ has knowingly accessed Heaven's Court to divorce herself from Baal—in other words, from her historic idolatry. This shift is prophesied in Hosea 2 as part of God's end-time drama. And it's a primary mandate for the bride to be received by her Bridegroom.

All that said, as watchmen our primary focus must continue to be real-time prophetic revelation more than end-time revelation. There's a big difference between the two. What is the Lord saying and doing right now?

Note that in Jesus' parable, the midnight rider received and conveyed real-time divine intelligence. Likewise as a covenant people, we must become aligned with His "now" timing. The reality is that as we move into the end times, real-time prophetic revelation from God's Throne is only going to increase. And again, each progression of His movement draws us closer to His ultimate approach.

Say you are traveling by car to Washington DC to visit the newly-opened Museum of the Bible. You set your GPS to map out the journey. You adjust your mirrors so you can accurately see what's behind. But your most intense focus must remain the road immediately in front of you.

It's important to look ahead. The Bible is your GPS, conveying both a long-term overview of your entire journey as well as real-time updates on the road immediately in front of you. Be flexible enough to embrace all course corrections that it brings.

That said—what do you see right now? If you can move with His Spirit in real-time revelation, empowered by a heart of love and obedience, you will naturally be positioned for the next phase of His journey.

Progressive Revelation—Bridegroom, Judge, King

Here's an example of how Jesus builds on revelation from season to season in order to propel His body forward. I want to propose to you that each decade of the previous 30 years has brought a new facet of revelation about Jesus—from Bridegroom to Judge to King. And each revelation has launched us into a new pioneering season.

Revelation—Jesus as Bridegroom, 1988-2001

In 2018 God is stirring the winds of revelation for us to again behold the countenance of Jesus as a Bridegroom to His people. In the 1990s this was a primary emphasis from the Throne. We began to relate to Jesus as a Bridegroom. We discovered His passionate devotion to us personally. We prayed the love language of the Song of Songs. Your love is more delightful than wine! The "Harp and Bowl" prayer movement was globally birthed out of this revelation.

Revelation—Jesus as Judge, 1999-2012

In the decade that launched the new millennium, the winds of revelation shifted. We began to perceive Jesus as Judge. Cutting-edge revelation poured in on how to approach the bench and receive real-time verdicts from Heaven's Court that brought immediate and lasting turnarounds.

You may not realize that the sweeping movement unveiling Jesus as Judge was primarily birthed out of the revelation of Jesus as Bridegroom. Our ultimate identity is as His bride. But we discovered that our condition was more like the compromised whore pictured in the Book of Hosea. Enslaved by the very lovers whom we thought would free us, we needed rescued!

Legally, to satisfy Heaven's Court, we needed a divorce from Baal. What followed was the largest and most comprehensive repudiation of idolatry in American history.

For us this project largely culminated on July 4, 2011, on the steps of the Lincoln Memorial. "God, grant us this divorcement from Baal. Grant us Your hand again in marriage, renewing our covenantal commitments from the founding of the land. And as a sign that You have heard us, crack the hard shell of demonic resistance over Washington DC!"

It was amazing how this cry was answered. Fifty days afterwards to the day, an unprecedented earthquake measuring 5.8 on the Richter scale rocked Washington DC. The Washington Monument cracked. Gargoyles toppled from the National Cathedral. And we knew that, in the midst of the quake, God had confirmed that His covenant had been restored.

Davids Tent, Museum of the Bible

Within a year two amazing events transpired in Washington DC. First, my friend Jason Hershey became inspired to launch 40 days of

24-7 worship in a tent on the White House Ellipse. David's Tent now welcomes Jesus to our nation's Capitol 24-7, 365 days a year on the National Mall.

The second amazing event was the launch of the Museum of the Bible—with Washington DC as its home! Again this occurred within a year of our covenant restoration. We immediately felt the Museum of the Bible was a representation of America's Ark of the Covenant. Such an honor to host Revolution 2017 there!

Revelation—Jesus as King, 2012-present

From that period on, fresh revelation of Jesus as King began to sweep through the body of Christ. The "Crown & Throne" prayer movement was birthed out of this revelation, conveying a dramatic progression into the Kingship anointing. We began to perceive how thrones of governance were tied to covenant. And the nation shifted accordingly. No King but Jesus!

> PROPHETICALLY, A NEW "TABERNACLES MOVEMENT" IS BEGINNING TO USHER IN GLOBALLY THE NEXT PHASE OF THE RESTORATION OF THE TABERNACLES OF DAVID.

At Faneuil Hall in 7-22, 2014, the Lord released what we now call His "Turnaround Verdict." From Daniel 7:22, a verdict of justice in favor of the saints, restraining the enemy and releasing the saints to possess the kingdom. Elections in both Israel and America, including the 2016 presidential elections, were dramatically impacted. A midnight turnaround! We'll share more on this later in the book.

We have begun to perceive Him as Judge, and now as King. What I want you to see, though, is how each ensuing season was actually sourced from our initial revelation of Jesus as Bridegroom. This is vital to understand. Because gaining a fresh vision of this Lover of your soul is key to unlocking the next wave of revelation the Lord wants to bring.

Behold the Bridegroom. He's coming! Rise up to meet Him.

Tabernacles Movement—5778

Our nation is now awakening and rising up. But where exactly are we going? This bridal procession has a destination! And scripturally, the journey of the bride culminates in a great celebration—under a bridal canopy.

Prophetically, a new "Tabernacles movement" is beginning to usher in globally the next phase of the restoration of the Tabernacle of David. This movement is prophesied in Amos 9:11-15. I don't believe it was any coincidence the Lord mandated that our own procession, a nationwide Glory Train journey, culminated at the 50 state, 50 tent "Awaken the Dawn" gathering. With 24-7 worship on the National Mall over the Feast of Tabernacles!

The Lord is tabernacling with us. In fact, Tabernacles 5778 launched His body into both our new year Hebraically, and a new season of revelation that will move us forward from now through 2020.

Even the Hebrew meaning of this new year symbolically conveys this movement. Here's just a taste. The number "8" is the Hebrew number "chet." The symbolism of this number conveys two meanings. First, it conveys a door or a gate. Second it conveys a bridal canopy. A tabernacle. So it's not a coincidence that as we entered into the Hebrew year 5778, the first major gathering of the body of Christ was a 50 state, 50 tent worship meeting on the National Mall!

Remember that to celebrate the Feast of Tabernacles, God originally commanded His people to convene in their nation's capital—Jerusalem—to worship the Lord in tents. The "Awaken the Dawn" gathering was one of the closest representations of God's original command seen since biblical days.

And again, it is a sign for us. A new tabernacles movement is forming. Our covenant restoration is going to be met with His tangible presence, personally and corporately. Burning lamps will be restored to the tabernacle. New wineskins are going to form to hold the best wine that Jesus has saved for last.

And over all, His glory is going to be a bridal canopy for His people!

Limited Window of Opportunity

That said, there's another message from the "midnight cry" we must take seriously this year. Because Jesus also warned that the door to His wedding ceremony would close very quickly. Please consider that the foolish virgins did not make it through the gate. They were shut out. And their only recourse was to try and take what the wise virgins had obtained.

At first Jesus' message seems way too abrupt, especially given the context. All are welcome at His wedding feast—after all, He died for us and rose again to secure our place by His side!

But there are also consequences to our actions. Jesus is warning us to set the course of our lives accordingly and redeem the time. Because an amazing door has now opened for us to secure our future. We've emphasized over and over again this window of opportunity is limited. We must fully give ourselves while it is at hand.

WE WILL SEE THE RESURGENCE OF A "BURNING LAMP MOVEMENT" THIS YEAR WHICH WILL EMPOWER THE PRAYER MOVEMENT... A MIDNIGHT CRY TO COUNTER A MIDNIGHT CRISIS

But how? First, Jesus emphasized it is important to buy oil now that will sustain your lamp in the future. Plan and prepare. Invest in the destiny you know the Lord has summoned you to fulfill. Let your seed set the course for your future. Sow to the Spirit, and you will reap a perpetual flow of provision to sustain you through the journey!

Second, as Jesus admonished, you must keep watch.

The Midnight Watch

Jesus opens His parable of the midnight cry by describing how the bridal party awakens and lights their lamps. An amazing, symbolic prophecy of a midnight watch in the midnight hours of history. A global prayer movement!

He closes this entire parable by describing this call to His disciples. Nobody knows the day nor the hour. Therefore keep watch!

Note that the watch portrayed in this parable was not actually initiated by the bridal party's awakening. Instead, the watch originated with a solitary forerunner who kept alert while others slept. He received the divine intelligence about God's timing. And he rode to convey the orders he received.

That's your invitation as well.

Again, I believe we will see the resurgence of a "burning lamp movement this year" which will empower the prayer movement to keep the watch Jesus is calling forth. A midnight cry to counter a midnight crisis.

Many are looking for signals, but perhaps a signal has already been sent. In 2007 James Goll released a profound book called Prayer Storm. He was commissioned by the Lord in a dream to relight and release the global Moravian lampstand. A global 24-7 watch of the Lord to counter the global end-time storms that would soon ensue.

Quite literally, a midnight watch.

The book and movement were both ahead of their time. To our amazement, James recently entrusted Jolene and me with the leadership of this movement. And I believe the imagery of a global Prayer Storm speaks more into the coming years than we could possibly imagine.

The Midnight Crisis

Here's some real-time divine intelligence regarding a midnight crisis. Just after Hurricane Harvey struck the shores of Texas, our friend Lynnie Harlow released the following word.

"On Monday night I had a dream. In the dream I was asking God to protect our President. I also asked him help our President start to say things more diplomatically. I heard God loud and clear tell me "NO" to the second one. He then said, "I am using the foolish things to confound the wise. And over the next 3 months there will be a huge shaking back to back to back on a National level.

"But then breakthrough WILL COME. And through the hard places a CRY will come forth in this Nation and the flood of MY spirit will not cease."

Lynnie prophesied huge shakings would occur back to back to back. Amazingly, after she prophesied this word two more hurricanes—Irma and Maria—formed and hit our nation. Along with Hurricane Harvey, they literally struck back to back to back.

It is amazing how prayer lessened the impact. I'll share one amazing story with you in a moment. But even after the storms, more shakings continued.

- North Korea successfully tested a hydrogen bomb, and then threatened to unleash hell on our land.

- A sniper in a Las Vegas resort hotel sprayed bullets into a crowd attending a country music concert, leaving 58 dead and 546 injured.

- Shakings in Hollywood exposed Hollywood gatekeeper Harvey Weinstein and his reprehensible legacy of sexual abuse.

- The reverberations continued in Washington DC with injustice and corruption being daily exposed at a level which made Watergate look like child's play.

- On October 31, ISIS struck our homeland. A terrorist rammed into a crowd of people, killing eight and wounding eleven. It was the largest known terror strike in New York City since September 11.

- At least 26 people were killed after a gunman entered a church service in a small town near San Antonio, TX. It was the worst shooting incident in Texas history. We are praying for the survivors.

Back to back to back. Seeing the accuracy of Lynnie's word, my greatest hope is that the rest of this prophetic promise will be fulfilled as comprehensively. Preferably immediately. Through the hard places a cry will come forth, and the flood of My Spirit will not cease.

What provokes the hand of God to move? What can lessen the impact of coming storms? More than anything, the cry of your prayers.

Countering a Category 5

Hurricane Irma was barreling towards Florida when my friend

Mario Bramnick, an apostolic leader from Fort Lauderdale, received an amazing assignment. He felt the Lord called him to remain and pray onsite. You might remember that Irma was a Category 5 hurricane, the strongest seen in the Atlantic in more than a decade.

And it was the second of the "back to back to back" hurricanes Lynnie Harlow had seen. Forecasters had predicted a direct hit for Mario's home.

My advice was to get out of there, and I even invited his family to fly to DC and stay with us. But he felt strongly to stay and keep watch! It was amazing to see how the storm suddenly shifted away from Florida. If it had remained only 20 miles to the east, most of the state would have literally been devastated. Instead the winds and rain caused only minimal damage.

PRESIDENT TRUMP WILL BE A WINSTON CHURCHILL FOR OUR TIME. THE MOST IMPORTANT QUESTION THEN BECOMES—WHY DOES AMERICA NEED A WINSTON CHURCHILL IN THIS HOUR?

What an incredible lesson for us all to learn. Note that I am by no means endorsing the idea of remaining onsite during a hurricane. But I am advocating a "prayer storm" to counter the coming storms.

Keep watch! Keep your lamp burning. Your midnight watch can absolutely lessen the impact of the storms of coming challenges. Or avert them all together.

White House Prayer

"Have you ever heard the story of the midnight cry? Like, with Paul Revere?"

Having just prayed through a hurricane, Mario Bramnick called me to get details on Lynnie Harlow's word. He had just heard in his spirit the phrase "midnight cry." As in the days of Paul Revere, there's a midnight crisis which provokes a midnight cry.

"I've heard something similar, my friend." He didn't know I had received two prophecies, one by Cindy Jacobs, prophesying that I was a "spiritual Paul Revere." More on that in a moment.

Mario's focus on a coming cry actually began in our home a few months before. Looking out our window at Washington DC, we spent some time praying in preparation for a meeting we were attending at the White House with a focus on mobilizing prayer.

Immediately the Lord began to quicken to him how circumstances must provoke a new level of prayer. A cry from His people. Mario even felt that President Trump was being invited to lead the way. This perception is already proving very accurate. From calling a national day of prayer to invoking God to overcome friction between nations, President Trump has led the nation in crying out to Jesus. We in turn must continue to pray for him!

President Trump is a revolutionary figure. From the beginning of his candidacy we've prophesied that he will be a Winston Churchill for our time. The most important question then becomes—Why does America need a Winston Churchill in this hour?

What exactly are we facing?

Maybe this is why the Lord is so emphasizing the midnight cry for 2018. Winston Churchill's fierce leadership through World War II was accompanied by a "burning lamp movement" of 24-7 prayer led by Welsh intercessor Rees Howells. I know the Trump administration desperately needs this magnitude of prayer as our nation confronts the challenges of our time.

We need a midnight cry... beginning at the White House!

The Midnight Riders

When Mario asked about Paul Revere, I almost mentioned the copy of our book "Crown & Throne" I had given him. It chronicles the rise and calling of a new breed of spiritual revolutionaries. Of course he read it. He probably just overlooked that part...

In case you missed it too, here's a recap of the story. Like many born in Massachusetts, I'm actually a direct descendant of one of the Pilgrims who signed the Mayflower Compact and committed this land and government to Jesus Christ. I am also a distant cousin of legendary patriot Paul Revere. His "midnight ride" launched the American Revolution—and birthed our nation.

Revere observed two lamps burning in the steeple of the Old North Church, signaling that a British invasion of Boston had commenced. He began a midnight ride through neighboring villages, awakening the local militias to fight with what became known as "the midnight cry."

Back in 1998, a prophetic word redefined my world. I had just hosted a conference in Boston's Faneuil Hall, known as the "womb of the American Revolution." I then flew to Kansas City for a conference. A prophet still unknown to me shared the following vision:

"You are a spiritual Paul Revere. I see you holding out a burning lamp, going from city to city. And instead of saying "The British are coming! The British are coming!" You are saying "the Lord is coming! The Lord is coming!"

The prophet had no idea my ministry was called Lamplighter, yet he saw me holding a burning lamp. Neither did he have any idea I had just held a conference in Boston's Faneuil Hall, the epicenter of Paul Revere's revolution.

A few years later Cindy Jacobs prophesied to me the very same mandate—literally almost word for word. How she does things like this, I still have no idea.

"You are a spiritual Paul Revere..." Cindy began. "I see you holding out a burning lamp, going from city to city. And instead of saying, "The British are coming! The British are coming! You are saying "the Lord is coming! The Lord is coming!"

She then added one simple phrase to this prophetic message. "And everywhere you go, revival is going to break forth."

Two different prophets, one unknown and one known worldwide, conveyed the same exact message to me, word for word. An amazing calling. But I simply could not grasp the full message or how to move forward with the calling. There were ministry schools for evangelists and pastors and the like, but where do you go for training as a spiritual Paul Revere?

I finally received a breakthrough in perception when the Lord spoke to me that He was raising up spiritual revolutionaries in this season. They do not fit in either the old season or the current season because they were born as forerunners of a new season. And when these forerunners ride, they will redefine their world.

Then one morning in 2001, more revelation came. I was seeking the Lord at the International House of Prayer in Kansas City at the time, and my Bible randomly fell open to Matthew 25. I made the wise choice to take the hint and read.

> "Then the kingdom of heaven will be comparable to ten virgins, who took their lamps and went out to meet the bridegroom. Five of them were foolish, and five were prudent. For when the foolish took their lamps, they took no oil with them, but the prudent took oil in flasks along with their lamps.

> Now while the bridegroom was delaying, they all got drowsy and began to sleep. But at midnight there was a shout, 'Behold, the bridegroom! Come out to meet him.' Then all those virgins rose and trimmed their lamps…" (Matthew 25:1-7).

To my astonishment, these words seemed to leap off the pages… and right into my mysterious prophecy! Matthew 25 actually conveys a midnight ride. With a midnight cry. And even a midnight awakening or revival! Further, this midnight rider was sent before Jesus to announce His coming.

And in response to the cry, the bridal party lit their lamps! As they awakened, they trimmed their lamps and went out to meet the Bridegroom. Which meant that the midnight rider who inspired them was actually a "Lamplighter."

I also immediately knew that many "lamplighters" were going to be raised up before the great midnight cry actually resounds. John the Baptist was a prototype of this calling, a "burning lamp" announcing Christ's first coming. Likewise in the end times, a great company of midnight riders, holding out their own burning lamps, will be sent before His face to crack the sky and announce His movement in the earth. Behold the Bridegroom!

And their midnight cry will summon multitudes to the wedding celebration.

Midnight Cry—A Christmas Story

The very end of this age culminates with a midnight cry. But it began with one as well.

Some two thousand years ago in Bethlehem, Israel, a pregnant teenager groaned while giving birth inside a darkened cave. Her burst of agony was immediately followed by the midnight cry of a newborn child as He drew His first breath on the earth.

Not far away, a few rugged herdsmen were keeping watch over their flocks. They followed in the footsteps of David, Israel's greatest shepherd, who once traversed these very same fields. The barren hillside was soon overtaken by a shining messenger. An angel of the Lord suddenly stood before them.

The manifest presence of God—His very glory—encompassed these shepherds like a fire. Even the fiercest feared for their lives, but no one dared run. No one dared even move.

> "But the angel said to them, "Do not be afraid; for behold,
> I bring you good news of great joy which will be for
> all the people; for today in the city of David there has
> been born for you a Savior, who is Christ the Lord. This
> will be a sign for you: you will find a baby wrapped
> in cloths and lying in a manger" (Luke 2:9-12).

This child in a manger was Israel's long awaited Messiah. The Son of David. Born in a midnight hour as the Light of the world!

The magnitude of this message must have seemed impossible to understand. But it was immediately backed by Heaven's visitation as thousands of heavenly hosts suddenly appeared, shimmering like lamps or lightning on the same barren hillside.

"Glory to God in the highest! And on earth, peace among men with whom He is pleased."

Following the angel's instruction, the shepherds embarked on a midnight journey to behold the newborn Child. A mother's groan, a baby's gasp, praises to God reverberating through the hills of Bethlehem as God's greatest gift was given to mankind.

For thousands of years since, the very echoes of this "midnight cry" have awakened our hearts. And they compel us to rise up and seek Him today.

CHAPTER TWO
Burning Lamp Awakening

Messiah's love is described as an unquenchable fire. Much of the prophetic imagery of both the Old and New Testaments conveys His fiery affection for His people. This unquenchable resolve even drove Him to the cross—and secured His resurrection. Jesus governs covenantally. And He gives Himself to His people covenantally, holding nothing back.

Throughout the Bible, fire is a symbol of God's covenant. A better way to put it is that fire is a seal of His covenant, an affirmation that His covenant blessings are either released or restored. Really the burning lamp symbolizes God's glory.

"Set me as a seal upon your arm, as a seal upon your heart. For love is as strong as death, its passion as unyielding as the grave. Its flashes are flashes of fire, the very flame of the Lord" (Song of Songs 8:6).

When the Lord came to Abraham, he cut covenant with Himself for the land and people Israel. The sign was a burning lamp. David, Solomon, and Elijah all saw fire fall from Heaven, sealing again God's covenant with Israel. Even the disciples experienced this in the upper room. Pentecost. Wind and fire. They experienced the literal restoration of God's glory.

And the Lord commanded that the fire on His altar never go out. It was to always be kept burning as a witness of His covenant love.

The Midnight Awakening

The midnight cry is a summons to a wedding. At the sound of the cry, the bridal party awakens and trims their lamps to go out and meet the Bridegroom. Passion for Jesus becomes reawakened. The flame of His love blazes. Symbolically, the prayer movement across the earth is re-ignited.

I cannot emphasize enough that this is happening right now. In the midst of this season's midnight crisis, God is granting a midnight awakening. God's glory is being progressively restored, even to you personally. No more delay!

So hear again the ageless cry. If it can awaken the bride in the midnight hour, it can awaken and ignite your heart as you step out on His word.

Behold the Bridegroom. He's coming. Rise up to meet Him!

Carriers of Covenant

As the bridal procession makes their midnight journey, they begin to shine their lamps in the streets with God's glory. They become carriers of covenant.

The Light of the World never intended for us to live without His glory defining us. But glory and covenant are joined together. He is a Bridegroom. And He reserves His most intimate blessing, personally and corporately, for those who fully embrace His covenant. No covenant, no glory! That's why David had to restore the Ark of the Covenant to welcome God's manifest presence into his capital city. He had to repair his nation's covenant with God.

> THE LIGHT OF THE WORLD NEVER INTENDED FOR US TO LIVE WITHOUT HIS GLORY DEFINING US

This is a mandate for today's forerunners too.

Burning Lamps

John the Baptist was known to Jesus as "the burning and shining lamp." As a "friend of the Bridegroom," he literally carried Christ's covenant by preparing the bride for His appearing.

The haunting imagery of the prophet Isaiah also conveys this process.

"For Zion's sake I will not hold my peace, and for Jerusalem's sake I will not rest until her righteousness shines forth like brightness, and her salvation as a lamp that burns. The nations will see your righteousness, and all kings your glory!" (Isaiah 62:1-2).

A lamp that burns. That's how I want to be known, how about you?

The Summons

Remember, the midnight cry is a summons to a wedding. Jolene and I didn't know each other yet; in fact we lived five states away from each other. I was a single dad. But in a midnight hour for each of us, Heaven's mysterious invitation would soon bring us together for a wedding. And a miracle during our ceremony would soon redefine our lives.

Jesus presented Jolene with a personal invitation to our wedding seven years before we met. I'm not kidding. Most likely she received the summons in a literal midnight hour too, because she received it in a dream.

Symbolically it was a midnight hour for Jolene. Like many single ladies, she had been praying diligently for a husband. But she was somewhat unique in that, when she rededicated her life to the Lord, He freed her from some very difficult entanglements and betrayal. The Lord asked her immediately to give up dating and simply wait on Him.

Jolene likes to say there was only one club she was still allowed to go to on Friday nights. That was Price Club (now Costco), and Jesus was the date!

It was tough for her. But one of the first things people notice about Jolene is that she is a woman of incredible integrity and resolve. In a short time she learned to relate to the Lord as her only needed companion. She even purchased a special ring to wear as a reminder of her covenant commitment—first to her Bridegroom Jesus, and then to the husband He had chosen for her.

It never came off her hand.

Jolene also prayed over her wedding, seeking foremost that the Lord would visit the ceremony with His presence. And that's when He visited her, seven years before we met, in a dream.

A beautiful wedding invitation was laying on a table. You could say it was a scroll. When Jolene looked closer, she discovered it was an invitation to her own marriage. She couldn't make out the name of the groom, the location of the wedding, or the year the ceremony would be held. The only thing clear in the invitation was her own name.

And a date. December 20. It was the only part of the invitation she could remember.

> ⟨!⟩
>
> IN A DREAM, A BEAUTIFUL WEDDING INVITATION WAS LAYING THE TABLE. WHEN JOLENE LOOKED CLOSER, SHE DISCOVERED IT WAS AN INVITATION TO HER OWN MARRIAGE.

Jon's Summons

Jolene and I met at a church picnic seven years later, in July 2003. As a single dad, a church picnic with a bunch of people I didn't know was the last place I wanted to be. Especially because they all seemed to know me—and my story.

My two kids and I had just moved to metro Washington DC from Kansas City to begin life again. As with many families, an unexpected betrayal had sent our lives crashing down.

In Kansas City, I was just beginning to find success in a ministry career when my own midnight hour came. Returning home from a conference in New England, I ran across a phone number I didn't recognize. So I hit the redial button. Turned out a call had been placed to an obscure hotel outside of town while I was away.

A little probing brought confirmation to my worst fears. For the third time, a vicious cycle of betrayal was poised blow our family apart. This time the marriage was irreparable. And I soon became a single dad with full custody—and full responsibility—for my kids.

In the very same season, my mom passed away suddenly from cancer. It seemed like our whole world was unravelling.

Shiloh Encounter—Summons from Heaven's Court

It was during this time that God intervened very dramatically in my life—and issued my own summons to Jolene and my wedding. I've shared this part of my story privately before, but never actually publicly until now.

Behind my home in Kansas City was a large park known locally as

Shiloh. Filled with trees, lakes and walking trails, Shiloh soon became my "secret place" of prayer as I walked through the agonizing process of divorce and transition. After taking care of things at home, I would often spend a few hours there just waiting on the Lord and praying for my son and daughter.

One afternoon I felt especially overwhelmed. My friend Will Ford, a minister in Dallas and later the best man at our wedding, helped pray me through. Will sounded like a broken record, and I told him so. Because over and over again he conveyed his sense that God was launching the kids and me into a new beginning.

After the call I decided to take a walk near a lake on the Shiloh property. As I approached the water I had a prophetic experience. It was more than a vision, because my eyes were wide open when it occurred.

All of the sudden I saw my former wife on my left side, and a woman in a wedding dress on my right side. Her face was veiled so I could not see her clearly. A long piece of wood formed a boundary in front of us. And I heard the Lord say, "take the hand of your new bride and cross the threshold into your new beginning."

Startled, I did as I was told.

Not knowing what to do next, I just thanked God for His new beginning and worshipped. Suddenly the words thundered, "Court of Heaven adjourned!" And what looked like a flood of angelic hosts shot up into Heaven.

What just happened! Was this even real? It was the first time I had ever heard the phrase, "Court of Heaven." Returning to the car, I called my friend Will again to try and process the experience. More for accountability's sake than anything else.

Will just laughed. "Hamill I told you so," he said. "God is launching you and the kids into a new beginning!"

You know, even after the divorce I had a hard time letting go. This prophetic experience became the reference point for the rest of my life. I am forever grateful for Will's prayers, which helped prepare the way for God's visitation.

Friends I'm sharing this portion of my story right now for a purpose.

If my story is similar to yours, please know that Lord intends for this experience to speak to you as well. Maybe your heart has been betrayed or maybe you've been abused. In order to cross the threshold into your new season, you will have to let go. You must forgive. And you will have to embrace the barrier the Lord intends to establish between your past and the future He intends for you.

A few of you who are reading this have been enduring abusive relationships involving prolonged, systemic betrayal. At your request, Heaven's Court can be convened over your situation. Verdicts can be rendered which will impact your world. Betrayal of covenant can be redemptively exposed. And new beginnings can come by God's hand—often in startling, unexpected ways.

> MAYBE YOUR HEART HAS BEEN BETRAYED OR MAYBE YOU HAVE BEEN ABUSED. IN ORDER TO CROSS THE THRESHOLD INTO YOUR NEW SEASON, YOU WILL HAVE TO LET GO. AND YOU WILL HAVE TO HONOR THE BARRIER THE LORD INTENDS TO ESTABLISH BETWEEN YOUR PAST AND THE FUTURE HE INTENDS FOR YOU

I strongly urge you to allow the Lord to be your defense. In other words, don't try to take matters into your own hands with harmful words or actions. Get people praying for you. Seek advice from trusted advisors, including competent ministry leaders. And let the Lord guide you through to the new beginning He intends for you.

A New Way Forward

My dad soon suggested that we join him and move to Frederick, Maryland, a small town 45 miles from Washington DC. He suggested we could rent a townhome together, a stable staging area for all of us to recover and start life over again. The area was known for top-rated schools and a strong job market. It seemed like a good opportunity.

Amazingly, my friend James Goll had just given me a prophetic directive—it was time to return to the east coast. I never pictured returning in this way though. Because of his word, I talked with James about my Dad's offer to bring our family together in Frederick Maryland.

An immediate, hopeful "yes" resounded from the other side of the phone line. James had just ministered in Frederick. He called his pastor friends there and filled them in, compelling them to care for us when we arrived.

Meeting at the Drink Table

All that said, I was still trying to make my way through the pain of the previous year when the church picnic came around. I originally declined when my new pastors asked me to attend. It was way too hard to socialize. But Jonathan and Ashley wanted to make new friends, and they begged me to go. Reluctantly I agreed.

This small decision turned out to be one of the most pivotal of my entire life.

Shortly after we arrived, my daughter Ashley, age 10, made a beeline to the drink table. While pouring a cup of soda, she actually made a new friend—just not from the age group I expected! Ashley somehow decided to strike up a conversation with an attractive, middle-aged prayer warrior. Jolene.

"Hey... have you met my dad yet?" Ashley asked her, bright-eyed.

"No, I haven't" replied Jolene politely. "But I have a feeling I'm about to."

Thanks to Ashley, Jolene and I got acquainted with each other over a cup of Coke. It was awkward for sure. But we soon discovered we got along really well. My daughter later told us that at the drink table, she looked for the prettiest girl she could find who wasn't wearing a wedding ring. Because she knew her dad needed a wife.

True story. And I could only concur on both counts.

Jolene invited me to the weekly prayer meeting she hosted each Thursday at her home. It was so different than the intercessory watches I was used to. There was no striving to "get God to come." Instead, divine presence and power saturated the meeting from the moment we began, without any striving. It amazed me how naturally she related to Jesus—devoted, personal, sincere, full of both intense resolve and gentle hilarity. It was clear she genuinely knew Him.

And I couldn't help but notice Jolene was beautiful. With warm brown eyes and a relentlessly mischievous smile, she was known as the "poster child of singlehood" at the church. One of the great mysteries of life was how she had not been spoken for already. What I didn't know was that the ring on her hand bore witness to her covenant commitment never to date until she found the right man. The one God had chosen for her.

The Date

One particular Thursday evening, most of Jolene's friends had begged off of her prayer meeting. They all had a good excuse—a hurricane was approaching. For some reason it didn't deter me though. In fact it inspired me. I literally raced through Frederick's flooded streets to get there.

Please note I was putting myself at great risk. Not because of the hurricane, but because of the keen discernment of the prayer meeting's host. I had already discovered that the overflow of Jolene's intimate relationship with Jesus made her naturally prophetic. She was supernaturally insightful about the hidden motivations of the heart.

Especially those who braved hurricanes just to be at her prayer gathering.

So to be safe, I waited a few days after the hurricane to ask Jolene on our first date. Amazingly, she said yes. I played it safe with TGI Fridays. By our second date I was pretty convinced she liked me. And by the third date I was pretty much head over heels for her. We climbed nearby trails together to see the fall foliage. It was the first time I ever held her hand.

An obvious question soon began to consume my thoughts. Is Jolene really the one? There was so much at stake—life, family, calling. I asked the Lord continually for His direction and waited. It came in a wild, wonderful, and unexpected way.

Our Engagement

My kids would often join me for the weekly prayer meeting at Jolene's townhome. So to protect their hearts, I had not told them we were dating. In fact I went to great lengths to remain covert. Nor had we told any friends from the church, except our pastors. We both felt we needed their advice and blessing from the very beginning.

Jolene and I had been dating about a month when the weekly prayer meeting was disrupted by a sudden flash of revelation. It came once again from my daughter Ashley. Suddenly she felt inspired to jump up on Jolene's lap. She then proceeded to tell everyone in the room, "Jolene is my mom in the spirit!"

The chatter stopped. People gasped. I did too. I could literally feel the laser-like gaze of every intercessor land on me. Then on Jolene. Then on my kids.

Jolene a mom? Was the church's poster child for singlehood actually dating? Was she actually dating Jon?

Someone finally broke the silence. "Well that's nice, dear. Everyone needs a spiritual mom, and you found yourself a good one."

Slowly the chatter picked up again. But there was no escape from this highly discerning crowd of seasoned intercessors. We were busted.

In protective mode, I internally asked the Lord if it was true. Was Jolene truly the woman He had chosen for me? Was she the mom He wanted for my kids? Holy Spirit's response to my desperate inquiry was both immediate and clear.

"I desire that Jolene be your wife for life."

Wife for life. That settled it all. We actually became engaged that very night. Because this proposal was so spontaneous, I did not have a ring to give her. So I gave her my most precious commodity at the time, a Jewish prayer shawl I had received on one of my ministry tours. It represented God's bridal canopy. It represented covenant. It was as close as I could come.

"I HAVE A GIFT FOR YOU." WITH GREAT CARE JOLENE SLID HER CONSECRATION RING OFF OF HER FINGER AND PUT ON MIND. TO BOTH OF OUR SURPRISE, THE RING JOLENE PURCHASED SEVEN YEARS AGO... WAS A PERFECT FIT.

Jolene then caught my attention with her beautiful eyes, now filled with tears. "I have a gift for you," she said. With great care Jolene slid her consecration ring off of her finger and put it on mine. To both of our surprise, the ring Jolene purchased seven years beforehand, as a sign of her covenant commitment to Christ and to the husband He had chosen for her, was a perfect fit on my finger.

I treasure this gift more than anything Jolene has ever given me. Of course, to this day it is my wedding band.

December 20

The next evening we began to dream together about our wedding. On a practical level, Jolene and I both agreed that a year-long courtship would be a great idea before getting married. This would carry us into fall 2004.

It was then that Jolene mentioned to me that the Lord had actually given her a special date for our ceremony. December 20. She explained that seven years ago, the date was highlighted in a dream in which she had received an invitation to her own wedding. My first thought was, "Who gets an invitation from the Lord to their own wedding?"

The advance planning was a bit unsettling. Heaven's wedding orchestrations for Jolene—and now me—were apparently much more advanced than I could have possibly imagined.

But when we checked our calendars, the date didn't line up with any kind of practicality for a Saturday wedding. December 20, 2004 fell on a Monday, not a Saturday—certainly out of the question for a wedding. In 2005, December 20 fell on a Tuesday. In fact, the only time December 20 fell on a Saturday was five long years away—certainly too long to wait.

To our shock there was actually only one Saturday which marked the convergence Jolene saw. December 20, 2003. It was only two months away. And it would make for exactly one month of courtship, followed by exactly two months of a whirlwind engagement.

But one further discovery tipped the scales in favor of the date. December 20, 2003 happened to mark the first day of Hanukkah, the Jewish holiday also known as the Feast of Dedication.

I was stunned.

As the founder of Lamplighter Ministries, this holiday had great meaning to me. Because Hanukkah celebrates the date a lamp was lit to reconsecrate the Jewish Temple to the Lord, after it had been desecrated.

The Hanukkah story is filled with miracles. To take back their Temple and light this lamp, the Maccabees had to overcome the strongest army in the entire Mideast. It was a miracle that they even survived.

Further, after relighting the menorah to restore their covenant with God, the Maccabees faced immediate burnout. Because they only had enough oil to keep it burning for a single day. Miraculously, the lamp blazed for eight days straight until fresh supply could be secured!

Lamplighter. Hanukkah. Lighting the lamp to mark a covenant dedication. New provision for a new beginning. Suddenly we both realized God was inviting us to take a major leap of faith, and hold our wedding on December 20. Only two months away.

When God invites us to immediate action, He has a miracle in mind. However, many times the baggage of our past experiences can cause us to hesitate, and therefore miss His opportunity. I am so glad Jolene and I decided to cross the threshold together. With the pain of our respective journeys, we both had major trust issues to overcome. But God helped us through the process.

And then He met us at our wedding in an unimaginable way.

Wedding Miracle on Hanukkah

Our wedding was planned out with great care. Since December 20 marked the first day of Hanukkah, we decided to make our "unity candle ceremony" the primary focus of our ceremony. We ordered a menorah from Jerusalem to hold the unity candle. To be accurate, it was actually a Hanukkiah, similar to a menorah but with nine candle holders instead of seven. It's used exclusively for the Feast of Dedication.

> WHEN GOD INVITES US TO IMMEDIATE ACTION, HE HAS A MIRACLE IN MIND. HOWEVER, MANY TIMES THE BAGGAGE OF OUR PAST EXPERIENCES CAN CAUSE US TO HESITATE, AND THEREFORE MISS THE OPPORTUNITY HE HAS CREATED FOR US.

Our plan was to worship, exchange our vows, then light this special menorah. The symbolic gesture would speak volumes. Lighting the candle together on Hanukkah to consecrate our marriage to the Lord and to each other.

The bridesmaids and groomsmen took their place. Jolene made her appearance at the back of the church. The poster child for singlehood looked absolutely stunning! The whole room became moved by her beauty and poise. Jolene's dad linked arms with her and escorted her on a tearful procession down the aisle. Right on cue, worship music began to fill the room—"Glory, glory, send your glory!"

Soon into our time of worship, my best man Will Ford elbowed me. I pretended not to notice. He nudged me again, and I looked over at him. For some reason, tears were streaming down his cheeks.

> TO OUR UTTER SURPRISE, OUR UNITY CANDLE WAS NOW AFLAME. YET NO HUMAN HAND HAD TOUCHED IT... GOD HIMSELF LIT THE UNITY CANDLE OF OUR MENORAH. ON THE FIRST DAY OF HANUKKAH

Will pointed over to the menorah. We had lit every candle except our unity candle, twice the size of the others. And our utter surprise that center candle was now aflame. Yet no human had touched it or had even come near.

God Himself lit the unity candle of our menorah, during our wedding ceremony. On the first day of Hanukkah. While we were singing "Glory, glory, send your glory." In front of everyone!

Just as He had promised, Jesus had come to Jolene and me during our wedding. He didn't ask permission. Nor did He even wait until the actual ceremony had begun. Instead, His presence became known as we welcomed Him in our worship. The fire lit. And all our friends and family experienced this miracle together.

Restoring Covenant, Redeeming Destiny

Neither Jolene nor I knew much about Jewish traditions when we were married, nor especially the Hebraic roots of our faith. We chose Hanukkah simply because God chose Hanukkah. Seven years before we met, through a midnight summons.

In retrospect, it was amazing to discover how our wedding story paralleled the miracle of this Feast of Dedication. Both of us had experienced severe betrayal earlier in our lives—the desecration of our "temple" by people closest to us. But God brought us into an incredible plan for restoration that redeemed many of the dreams and promises we had lived for, and even gave our lives for.

When God lit our lamp in our midnight hour, He awakened our hearts. He also redeemed our destiny.

Obviously a first priority for both Jolene and me was to find a faithful spouse. But more, we both longed for a genuine companion to journey through life with—equally yoked with Jesus, loving Him and loving each other. Sometimes we have our moments. But after fourteen years I still can't wait to spend every moment of the day with my bride.

When we married, my kids also found a mom. Thrust into parenthood after 43 years as a single girl, Jolene proved amazingly capable in bringing both nurture and much-needed course corrections to get Jonathan and Ashley on track for their future.

> BOTH OF US HAD EXPERIENCED SEVERE BETRAYAL EARLIER IN OUR LIVES... WHEN GOD LIT OUR LAMP IN THE MIDNIGHT HOUR, HE AWAKENED OUR HEARTS. HE ALSO REDEEMED OUR DESTINY. HE CAN DO THE SAME FOR YOU!

One of the biggest dreams Jolene and I both carried in our hearts was to fulfill the ministry calling the Lord placed on our lives. In my midnight hour, I had almost come to believe Lamplighter Ministries was a thing of the past. But amazingly, God relit our lamp.

And five years after our wedding, the Lord called us both out of the marketplace and into full-time ministry.

Here's my point in all of this. Maybe it seems your dreams have died. Or worse, maybe it seems that the innermost chambers of your heart are now beyond recovery. Beloved, God's plan for your restoration is so much bigger than you realize! You can begin again. You can feel again. You can love again. You can genuinely live again. You can fulfill your God-given dreams.

Jesus is all about new beginnings. Just as with the miracle of Hanukkah, the process starts with reconsecrating your life to Him. Take a few moments to pray.

Father God, thank you for your invitation to redeem my life. I consecrate myself to You right now—giving You my past, my present, my future, my hopes and dreams, my life. Light the fire in my heart again! Please heal the broken places of my spirit, soul and body. Show Yourself to me. Forgive me where I've wounded others, and restore me where others have wounded me.

Thank You for sending Jesus to fully redeem me. I believe Jesus took the punishment for my sins on the cross, fully paying the price for my new beginning. By His own blood, I now receive Your covenant with me, and Your destiny for my life. Help me to know you more and obey you fully. Grant me this new beginning right now, in Jesus' Name.

Do you want the fire sustained? Resolve to put Jesus first in your life and keep covenant with Him. Be a person of integrity. You will find that your new beginning will continue to be supernaturally empowered. He will never turn on you, get tired of you or abandon your heart. He offered His own life to gain your companionship. And your affection, your heart, your presence will never ever be taken for granted.

Vision: Jesus Tending Our Lampstand

It seems only right to close this chapter with a recent vision which made His care for us very real.

Though I've had many prophetic experiences, to my knowledge Jesus Himself has only appeared to me twice in the 30 years I've been walking with Him. The first time was in 2002. The second time was more recently, in January 2014, when I awoke from sleep to the vision below.

Jesus was dressed in a deep red robe, holding a menorah. It was barely burning. This flickering menorah was the only light that illuminated Him.

Jesus cradled the menorah in His hands, very close to His heart, and then wept into it. As His tears and breath fell upon the fire, the lamp literally began to blaze.

Jolene and I were attending "Holy Spirit Over Metro DC," a key regional conference at the time. And it's clear the vision was conveying

Holy Spirit's work in metro Washington DC and many other regions. He was tending our corporate lampstands, the light against the darkness, which were in danger of flickering out.

But the vision of Jesus cradling our menorah first represented Jolene and me, and our personal lampstand. He cares far more deeply about our personal first-love devotion than we could ever imagine. He wants our affection to shine!

And like a lover's gaze towards her beloved, that shining brightens His own countenance.

First Love Fire

In Revelation, Jesus is pictured standing among the lampstands when He gives the following admonition:

> "…You have perseverance and have endured for My name's sake, and have not grown weary. But I have this against you, that you have left your first love. Therefore remember from where you have fallen, and repent and do the deeds you did at first; or else I am coming to you and will remove your lampstand out of its place—unless you repent" (Revelation 2:3-5).

I am so grateful that Jesus Himself is holding your lampstand close and tending it with such care in this hour. All that the lampstand represents—passion and intimacy with Him, Throne Room access and ministry effectiveness, even regional breakthrough—He is desiring to preserve. He's making every opportunity available to you and me for this preservation.

But your response is needed. This warning about our priorities must be taken seriously.

But there's also a promise with the warning. I experienced first-hand how the same God of our first-love devotion has committed Himself to work with us and preserve this fire longterm. As you realign your priorities, He will reset your lampstand and relight the flame.

Here's a secret to keeping your fire burning. If your eye is single, your body is full of light. The enemy has tried to divide and scatter many of you in 2016 and 2017. Therefore the Spirit's work for 2018 begins with restoring your focus on Jesus. From this you will find the fire of your passion ignited again. A burning lamp awakening!

CHAPTER THREE
The Hanukkah Revolution

"It's closed, honey, it's closed! The restaurant is closed!" After our Hanukkah wedding, Jolene and I chose the Outer Banks of North Carolina for our honeymoon. It was amazing to spend our first Christmas together at a romantic cottage by the sea. At least until it came time for the holiday dinner. It seemed the only place open on Christmas was a convenience store.

Candy cane cappuccinos from 7-11 in hand, we stared despondently through the decorated windows of adorable, darkened restaurants. Closed for Christmas. Thank God we eventually found a solitary Chinese food restaurant ready to serve. Po Po platter on an open fire. Crab legs nipping at your nose. Comfort and joy in our time of peril!

Thus began a Christmas tradition we still hold dear, to this very day. Chinese food. Preferably a buffet.

Tradition is a big word for Christmas, isn't it? Some traditions—like home, hearth and family, egg nog and egg drop soup—are valid and worth preserving over generations. But some beliefs and traditions need to be evaluated.

Christian tradition holds that Jesus was born on December 25. This is largely thanks to the Roman emperor Constantine, who wanted to combine the Christian cerebration of Jesus' birth with two pagan winter celebrations popular during his time. In retrospect, he started what became Christianity's greatest holiday celebration with a lie—or at least a severe miscalculation.

Jesus was most likely born during the Feast of Tabernacles. This is the conclusion of many Messianic Jewish scholars who have thoroughly studied Jewish history and tradition as well as gospel accounts of the Christmas story. Key details from scripture support this. For instance, few shepherds would have imperiled their flock by pasturing the animals on a cold December night—especially since it's also Israel's rainy season.

PONDER THIS A MOMENT. THE LIGHT OF THE WORLD, THE LIFE THAT LIGHTS ALL MEN, WAS MOST LIKELY CONCEIVED OVER HANUKKAH! AND THE DARKNESS STILL HAS NO CAPACITY TO OVERCOME THIS DIVINE FIRE

With the rain and cold, it's also very doubtful King Herod would have imposed a census in December either—especially mandating national travel. But at Tabernacles, Jewish families traveled across the land to gather with their respective tribes and worship the Lord together. This would make a "tribe by tribe" census much more practical to administrate.

So if the conclusion of these researchers is true, again Jesus—God with us—was probably born around the Feast of Tabernacles. Which means He was actually conceived around the time we celebrate Christmas today.

Hanukkah. The Feast of Dedication. The Festival of Lights.

The Christmas Spirit is Hanukkah's Flame

Ponder this a moment. The Light of the World, the life that lights all men, was most likely conceived over Hanukkah! And the darkness still has no capacity to comprehend or overcome this Divine fire.

The implications of Yeshua being conceived over Hanukkah are startling. First, as the Light of the Word, the Jewish Messiah not only embodies both Hanukkah and Christmas; He fulfills them both.

Second it means that again, for 1700 years, ever since the Roman ruler Constantine shifted the church from her Jewish roots, we have most likely been celebrating Christ's birth during the time of His actual conception.

Ever wonder where God stands on pro-life issues? Maybe this strange reality, that the whole world celebrates Christmas at the time Jesus was actually conceived, is actually a coded communication meant to prophesy to our generation. Life not only begins at conception, but should be celebrated from conception.

All this said, some point to pagan influences as a reason not to celebrate Christmas. I disagree. I believe we actually need to restore the true Spirit of Christmas in our culture, with a clear focus on celebrating Jesus. But we also need to expand our celebration to embrace Hanukkah as a source. Lets ask God to divorce us from the pagan roots of Christmas and restore us to our covenant roots which actually make the celebration genuine—and even more beautiful.

Because scripturally, the true "Spirit of Christmas" is Holy Spirit. And the Christmas Spirit is actually Hanukkah's flame.

Beloved, this understanding also realigns our expectations for the season with the true heart of Heaven. It becomes all the more a season of warmth, of light, of fire and family. A beautiful time to spread your love by giving gifts and sharing meals.

But it also becomes a season of Holy Spirit visitation. Further, it becomes a season of conception by the Spirit which unlocks the harvest of your future.

Conceiving Fire

Remember God's love is compared to a flash of fire, His covenant to a burning lamp. It's only fitting that the Light of the World was conceived into the earth during the Festival of Lights. And it's only fitting that the Bridegroom—born to exchange His life for His bride—would be conceived during the Feast of Dedication.

The lamp of covenant relit. A desecrated Temple rededicated. A new beginning launched. Jesus, the Light of the world, won this opportunity for all humanity.

In Jesus' parable of the midnight cry, the virgins are all sent to carry His fire to the wedding feast. But a young virgin named Mary, or more accurately Miriam, was chosen by God to actually conceive His holy fire and birth Him into the earth.

> "The angel answered and said to her, "The Holy Spirit will come upon you, and the power of the Most High will overshadow you; and for that reason the holy Child shall be called the Son of God" (Luke 1:35).

God wants you to be like Mary. Authentic ministry is not so much sourced from the lamp in our hands, but the fire in our hearts. When you conceive His word, you conceive His fire. And this fire is not so much spread as it is birthed into our world.

Again, the true Christmas Spirit is Hanukkah's flame. Through Christ's conception over Hanukkah, the Lord Himself is drawing attention to the legacy of covenant rededication to God, divorced from all idolatry. Small wonder so many men and women dedicate their lives to Christ during this holiday season.

The Lord is also drawing our attention to the legacy of the courageous example of spiritual revolutionaries who upended the globalist structure of their day to restore their desolate heritage and launch their people into a new beginning.

Hanukkah celebrates the rise of spiritual revolutionaries. Of which Jesus, Redeemer of mankind, is the greatest who ever lived.

Jesus, Revolutionary

Jesus was born to redeem the world from the corruption of idolatry and sin. But His calling as a geopolitical revolutionary is not so much understood. His mother perceived this calling very clearly though. "He has brought down rulers from their thrones," she exclaimed about this babe while He was still in her womb. And has exalted those who were humble" (Luke 1:52).

Did you know that's part of Christ's calling—judging the nations, and bringing unjust rulers down from their thrones? That's revolutionary— and not very comfortable for most people. Ultimately Hanukkah even speaks into the final moments of the end-times, with Christ the King bringing down an antichrist ruler whom the Bible prophesies will set up his throne on the Temple Mount.

Hanukkah, the date of Christ's conception, is a literal prototype of this ultimate victory.

The Hanukkah Revolution

It was a midnight hour for Israel. In the first century BC, God's covenant land and people were held captive by a vicious globalist empire intent on removing from their culture any remembrance of the Jewish heritage or faith. Greece and Syria, both renown for their brutality, formed an alliance rooted in their idolatry. Together they sought to overtake the known world.

Antiochus IV Epiphanes was the ruler of the Greco-Syrian empire at the time of the Hanukkah revolution. Theologians today actually regard the man as a prototype of the antichrist. In any case, the Jewish resistance proved more formidable than anticipated. So Antiochus drew up plans to completely demoralize God's covenant people. He forbade them from celebrating their feasts, or even following their sacred law. Instead the value system forged by Greece and Syria was imposed on every aspect of their lives. They were even forced to violate their marriage laws.

But much of the cultural imposition was not imposed upon the Jewish people so much as it was welcomed. Israel's economy flourished as merchandise and trade increased exponentially. The introduction of new technology brought great enrichment to all aspects of life. A sect of Jews called "Hellenists" pointed to these benefits and compelled fellow Israelites to embrace all aspects of Greco-Syrian intentions.

GLOBALISM THEN AND NOW OFTEN WEARS A VERY BENIGN MASK— CENTERED ON THE EMPOWERMENT OF HUMANITY. THAT'S THE WAY IT WAS WITH THE GREEKS TO THE ROMAN EMPIRE, ALL THE WAY TO THE THIRD REICH

Globalism then and now wears a very benign mask—centered on the empowerment of humanity. That's the way it was with the Greeks and the Roman Empire all the way to the Third Reich and globalist efforts today. There's a difference between globalism and global engagement—empowered by Jesus Christ—which empowers genuine freedom to nations.

Warning! Idolatry remains at the core of globalism. And if embraced, the results will ultimately be devastating.

Further, you will find that the globalist agenda ultimately includes overtaking the Temple and setting up an antichrist throne. As an act of finality, Antiochus laid siege to the Temple Mount and captured God's holy sanctuary. The lamp was snuffed out. Offerings ceased, at least to the God of Israel. Instead, the Temple of God became ritually dedicated to occult powers—Zeus to the Greeks, Baal to the Syrians. On December 25, 168 BC Antiochus IV Epiphanes even dared to sacrifice a pig on the holy altar of God.

Beloved, it's never a good idea to pick a fight with the God of Israel. He never forsakes His covenant. And He never loses a battle. He judges and makes war.

With the plundering of the Temple, a small band of spiritual revolutionaries were awakened. They soon confronted the strongest army in the known world—and won.

These spiritual revolutionaries were known as Maccabees, Hammers. They were named after their founder Judah Maccabee, or "Praise Hammer." And against all odds, they broke through the battle lines of the Greco-Syrian army and retook their lost heritage. As you now know, the Maccabees sought to rededicate the Temple to the Lord by relighting His lampstand, the menorah. And as you know, it marked a new beginning for the Jewish people.

Could America Receive a New Beginning?

As Jolene and I moved forward in our calling, we began to realize just how desperate the situation in our nation really was. America was in a midnight hour where we as a nation could go either way. And Hanukkah's message of covenant restoration actually became a revolutionary prototype for us, to see the Lord redeem our nation and grant us a new beginning.

I saw how leaders during other low points in America's history had gained the same resolve as Judah Maccabee. Revere and his patriots defied all odds when they awakened to confront the British invasion. Francis Scott Key literally watched and prayed through a midnight battle for Baltimore, searching for our flag by dawn's early light. Abraham Lincoln saw the division in our nation, and concluded that only a miracle similar to a born-again experience could preserve our land. "That this nation under God shall have a new birth of freedom— and that government, of the people, by the people, and for the people, shall not perish from the earth."

A new beginning, forged by covenant restoration to preserve our freedom. God had granted this miracle in other times of American history. Why not now?

Prophecy—Judah Maccabee

"God is changing your name. You are now Judah Maccabee, Praise Hammer!" The words from apostolic leader Sandy Newman froze me in my tracks. In part because she was swinging a hammer in very close proximity while prophesying to me.

Over the years I've acquired some wisdom. For instance, never underestimate the power of a prophet with a hammer. Especially one who is so small in frame but so much larger than life.

> LIKE THE MACCABEES WE SAW THAT, FOR AMERICA'S RESTORATION, WE NEEDED TO SEPARATE OUT FROM A LONGSTANDING STRUCTURE OF IDOLATRY THAT WAS HOLDING BACK GOD'S INTENTIONS

The date was 12-12-12, and I had been asked to share on our Hanukkah journey with colleagues at our yearly HAPN/RPN prayer network conference in Oklahoma City. Sandy had purchased this hammer as a gift for me, and was presenting it on stage.

The parallels between the Hanukkah revolution and our project to divorce Baal were extraordinary. Separation and dedication are at the core of the Maccabee miracle which became Hanukkah. They relit the menorah in order to reconsecrate the Temple to God after it had been dedicated to demonic powers. Like the Maccabees we saw that, for

America's restoration, we needed to separate out from a longstanding structure of idolatry that was holding back God's intentions for our land.

Any covenant rededication must therefore include governmentally annulling all covenants with idolatry or pacts with demonic powers that had been previously established.

I'll share more on this in future chapters. But in short, we needed to divorce Baal.

Prophecy—Paul Revere and the Continental Congress

We also realized that, like the Maccabees, we needed to convene together as an army to mobilize towards the impossible breakthrough we dreamed of. The Lord brought to mind a prophetic word which Jill Austin gave to Jolene and me back in the summer of 2006.

Jill was a powerful prophet and a dear friend. Signs, wonders, and incredible moves of the Spirit accompanied her ministry everywhere she went. And so when Jill Austin prophesied a new move of God to us, we took notice.

"You are generals in the body of Christ!" Jill thundered. "You are like Paul Reveres. Revolutionaries. And God is calling you to convene a Second Continental Congress that will set a new way forward even for this nation. Because Jesus is always revolutionary. And He is bringing a new move of awakening and revival... a spiritual revolution!"

Jill Austin became the third prophet to call me a Paul Revere. And as best I recall, she was the first to use the phrase "spiritual revolution." With all the Lord had shown me personally, that really got my attention. Not long after, Jill passed on suddenly and unexpectedly. Her prophetic word on the Continental Congress turned out to be the last she would ever give us.

Keep in mind I was working full-time for the Department of Homeland Security at the time. I had no real desire to return to ministry at a concentrated level. But things changed at the word of the Lord. And just a year later, the Lord spoke to us to step into full-time ministry. It was one of the hardest decisions I had ever made because I loved my job so deeply. When I inquired of the Lord, He said simply, "The nation needs you." And I remembered Jill's prophecy. A decade later I guess I'm beginning to understand why.

Launching a Continental Congress

For many years we prayed into Jill's prophecy. The Lord began to connect us with friends known and unknown who had received similar words, including Abby Abildness of Healing Tree International in Hershey, PA and Jamie Fitt of the Philadelphia Tabernacle of David. In 2013 we felt to move forward together, committing to five years of annual Revolution gatherings which we dreamed would set a new course for the future.

Jamie Fitt brings the heartbeat of God to our team. Jamie is one of only a few worship leaders I know who flows in real-time prophetic revelation with a tangible governmental anointing for breakthrough. It is an amazing gift. I wrote about this aspect of worship in our book "Crown & Throne," and Jamie immediately adopted it. He is now pioneering a "Crown & Throne" worship movement.

Abby Abildness is one of the most effective pioneers in Kingdom diplomacy that I know. For decades, Abby's heartbeat has been to see the dream of Pennsylvania founder William Penn realized in this hour. Penn lived and died to forge an expression of Kingdom governance rooted in God's love, justice, and freedom.

Penn's doctrine was largely based on two principles. First, no king but Jesus. He invested His life for us! And therefore Jesus alone is worthy of the thrones of our hearts and the thrones of our governance.

Secondly, no cross, no crown. Only governmental leaders who follow the footsteps of Jesus by laying down their lives for their constituents are worthy to wear the crown and rule.

It's not a coincidence that the government of our nation was later framed in Philadelphia, PA. Our nation's foundational documents, including the Declaration of Independence and the US Constitution, are rooted in Penn's deepest convictions of freedom governance.

Our team knew the Lord desired to connect the original roots of freedom governance from Pennsylvania to Washington DC so as to restore our land according to the Founders' original intentions. During the Continental Congress, representatives of the original 13 Colonies gathered together many times in Philadelphia—first to break from England and fight a revolution, then to frame a new form of governance that would deliver the power back to the people and perpetuate genuine liberty generationally.

The Revolutionaries would rush into battle with the cry, "No King but Jesus!" And as we sought to shift our government back into the original intent for freedom, that became our midnight cry too.

Launching a Revolution

And we knew it would be a battle, just like Jill prophesied. Literally a Revolution. God was launching a Kingdom revolution to preserve the lamp of freedom our forefathers had entrusted to this nation.

Not coincidentally, our first book "Crown & Throne: a Field Guide to Spiritual Revolution" was launched during the first Revolution gathering. We noted in its pages that nobody fights a revolution just to take ground. Instead every revolution is fought to establish new government. Little did I know it would soon become a prophetic blueprint for the revolutionary governmental turnaround we are now living out. So much of it only makes sense in retrospect, especially after the 2016 elections.

Because we were engaging in a spiritual revolution, it only seemed right to begin our Revolution gatherings at Valley Forge, the Philadelphia suburb which hosted the ragtag continental army over a brutal winter in 1777-8. It was during this winter at Valley Forge that the eclectic collection of farmers and tradesmen, bankers and dockworkers and merchants trained and transformed into soldiers. Much like the Maccabees, they soon became capable enough to take on the mightiest army in the known world—and win.

We drew from the anointing of this hallowed ground. Because like our forefathers, we needed this magnitude of transformation to win the revolution of our time. A similar tenacity and growth in competence were both desperately needed. But above all else, Heaven's favor needed be secured.

Our annual Revolution gatherings soon became a Continental Congress for this hour. We convened mostly over Hanukkah, both to be trained and to stand as representatives in order to set a new course together. It was amazing to discover the extraordinary power of an ekklesia, a governmental representation of the body of Christ.

As you will see throughout the pages of this book, prophetic direction and substantive miracles have redirected our lives and even national governance from the precipice of disaster. By God's grace alone we have forged a new way forward for our land. And most amazingly, over and over again the tracks have been laid through spontaneous prophetic expressions during these gatherings.

As a result of our work in Christ, as well as the tireless dedication of many other movements, America received a new birth of freedom in the midst of our midnight hour. What an honor to celebrate by bringing Revolution 2017 to the newly-opened Museum of the Bible in Washington DC! We see it as America's Ark of the Covenant. And it's the perfect setting to honor the covenant which has preserved our land. Always remember that the midnight cry is a summons to a wedding.

More on this in the next few chapters. That said, we pray that this miracle not only continue, but greatly expand. Especially to you. As you read how impossibilities have turned into miracles in our day, may you be inspired to risk it all for the dream in your heart for the Lord.

Like the Maccabees and Miriam and all the spiritual revolutionaries who have gone before you, it's time to conceive holy fire. And then birth a revolution which will redefine your world. No King but Jesus!

By My Spirit—The Maccabee Miracle

Lets now examine the miracle that has actually come to define the holiday we know as Hanukkah. Not only was the fire relit, it was supernaturally sustained. And if it happened in their day, it can definitely happen in yours.

When the Maccabees reconsecrated the Temple to the Lord by relighting the menorah, they were consumed by the resolve of their forefathers that the fire on the altar must never go out. But they soon discovered they had no provision to keep the fire burning.

The Temple storehouse had been plundered. The supply of oil was gone. The Maccabee revolutionaries discovered they only had enough oil to sustain the fire for a single day.

Have you ever been there on your journey with God? You experience an initial breakthrough, only to encounter an even greater impossibility than what you and God just conquered.

That's the way it was for the Maccabees. After their first miracle, it seemed like their journey of restoration had come to a sudden end.

The Wise Store Oil

Oil has brought the rise and fall of nations and kingdoms. As a commodity it helped topple Soviet Russia, and then became the blood which was pumped into that same nation's veins to secure its amazing resurgence. Many nations, especially in the Mideast, live and die by this commodity. It's the mainstay of their economies.

In America and the western world, oil in its many forms runs our cars, heats our homes, soothes and perfumes our bodies, preserves our food and secures our retirement accounts. It even still fuels our lamps.

The primary benefit of oil is that it burns well. Jesus made this commodity a central issue of His parable of the ten virgins—the parable of the midnight cry. He demands we prepare, and then tells us how to prepare, for the unpredictable journey ahead.

Take oil. A midnight vigil is coming. And like the Maccabees, we need fresh oil to sustain our fire. Otherwise we too face the prospect of simply burning out.

Burning the Midnight Oil

You can probably imagine the Maccabee prayer meeting over their lack of oil. Remember, they were in the Temple they had just rescued from the tyrants. As the fire of their menorah dimmed, they cried to the Lord for help.

"Lord we want to establish your covenant! Remember the covenant promise you gave to Solomon on this very ground—that now your eyes will see, and your ears will hear, and your heart will be attentive to the prayers made here. We want to follow your ordinances, but we need a miracle to make it through. Lord give us oil! Grant us provision. For the sake of Your great Name, You must come through."

You can imagine the swirl in the spiritual realm. Heaven and earth must have become intensively focused. They were praying God's heart, His covenant. And because of this, the answer came.

I can imagine an angel of the Lord tapping Judah Maccabee on the shoulder. An unperceived whisper became interpreted as a very insightful thought. "Judah, remember the burning menorah. Not by might nor by power, but by My Spirit, says the Lord."

Of course. Zechariah 4. The prophet awakened and saw a golden lampstand being resourced by a perpetual flow of oil from two olive trees. It was a sign that the Temple restoration the God of Israel had desired will now be completed.

And Judah suddenly realized he had just become part of this very prophecy.

Miraculously, the flame kindled by the Maccabees never went out—even though the oil should have run dry the very first day. The flame burned miraculously for eight days straight until fresh oil could be secured. For this reason, over thousands of years Hanukkah has always been celebrated by lighting the candles of the lamp each night over an eight day period.

And also for this reason, from the time of her miraculous rebirth, the menorah became Israel's national symbol. With the braces of two olive trees surrounding it.

Beloved, nothing ignites the lamp of faith like discovering your own dream is recorded in God's word. There's a security that comes. You realize your calling is actually sourced from another realm—an unshakable throne with limitless provision.

And when you are stretched beyond capacity, when you're burning the midnight oil, you can dare to dream God's dream and through faith receive His provision.

Persevere! Pray and stand until God comes through. You have no idea how your miracle will speak to generations to come.

Burning Lamp Awakening—Another Picture

The prophet Zechariah is a harbinger for our period of history. We launched "Crown & Throne" five years ago during our first Revolution gathering, with the Holy Spirit emphasizing Zechariah 3 as a prototype for the hour. We are launching the "Midnight Cry" with the Holy Spirit emphasizing Zechariah 4 as a prototype prophetic word for 2018-2020.

NOTHING IGNITES YOUR LAMP OF FAITH LIKE DISCOVERING HOW YOUR OWN DREAM IS RECORDED IN GOD'S WORD. YOU REALIZE YOUR CALLING IS ACTUALLY SOURCED FROM ANOTHER REALM— AN UNSHAKEABLE THRONE WITH LIMITLESS PROVISION.

In Matthew 25, Jesus conveys how a midnight cry awakens His covenant people to ignite their lamps. This chapter in Zechariah also pictures a "burning lamp awakening." A prophecy to governmental leaders that it is time to complete the dream God forged in their hearts. Lets look at the passage.

"Then the angel who was speaking with me returned and roused me, as a man who is awakened from his sleep. He said to me, "What do you see?" And I said, "I see, and behold, a lampstand all of gold with its bowl on the top of it, and its seven lamps on it with seven spouts belonging to each of the lamps which are on the top of it; also two olive trees by it, one on the right side of the bowl and the other on its left side."

Then I said to the angel who was speaking with me saying, "What are these, my lord?" So the angel who was speaking with me answered and said to me, "Do you not know what these are?" And I said, "No, my lord."

Then he said to me, "This is the word of the Lord to Zerubbabel

saying, 'Not by might nor by power, but by My Spirit,' says
the Lord of hosts. 'What are you, O great mountain? Before
Zerubbabel you will become a plain; and he will bring
forth the top stone with shouts of "Grace, grace to it!"'"

Also the word of the Lord came to me, saying, "The hands
of Zerubbabel have laid the foundation of this house,
and his hands will finish it. Then you will know that the
Lord of hosts has sent me to you" (Zechariah 4:1-9).

Note that the angel of the Lord who had previously spoken to
Zechariah returned and awakened him from slumber. He then saw a
burning menorah. This is so similar to the experience of the midnight
rider and the bridal party. Through this the Lord not only awakened
the prophet, but I believe He also awakened the words and dreams
deposited in the prophet's heart during the former season.

Because the time had now come to complete the dream. Here's
Zechariah 4, Jon's translation:

"I am awakening you and showing the burning lamp to you as a sign
that the Temple will indeed be restored. By this you will complete the
dream I have given you in a former season.

"But the fire you see burning on the menorah does not require
natural oil, Zechariah. My anointing pours into this lamp night and
day. The might of armies cannot ignite its flame, nor can their supposed
power quench it. My Temple will be redeemed, and it will be finished,
in context with this burning lamp. Not by might nor power. But by My
Spirit, says the Lord!"

Remember that for believers, the only oil that can sustain our hearts
and lives is actually the anointing of God's Spirit. Just as with the
miracle of the Maccabees, He has the capacity to keep our fires burning
bright. But He also warns that some lampstands will go dark in the
midnight hour. I don't want yours to be among them.

Lets pursue God and be supernaturally sustained by His presence.
Lets receive His provision. Jesus will light your lamp. Again, as long as

you're willing, the covenant flame He has kindled in your heart will be protected and viably sustained. And the restoration mission you have carried in your heart will be completed. —X

Not by might nor by power, but by My Spirit says the Lord of hosts!

Covenant Wealth

Remember God gives power to gain wealth to establish the covenant He swore to our forefathers (Deuteronomy 8:18). As you align with His covenant, He will release both the wealth of Heaven and the provision of earth to sustain you and perpetuate your flame. It is sacred to Him just as it is sacred to you. And the fire on the altar must never go out; it is to always be kept burning!

Many will find this two-year period from 2018-2020 to be an incredible season for wealth generation. God is releasing covenant wealth so that His covenant may be established in America and among the nations of the earth. A burning lamp awakening!

I love the orchestrations of God. Because November 11, 2020 marks the 400th anniversary of the signing of the Mayflower Compact by the Pilgrims. Remember the Jews were held captive in Egypt for 400 years when God "remembered His covenant" and launched a revolution for their freedom. I prophesy to you, by the Spirit of God, that God is moving in a similar way now to bring His people across the nation and world into freedom! As chronicled in Crown & Throne, He is releasing a global Moses movement to counter the global Pharaoh movement which seeks to usurp God's covenant plan.

And He's releasing covenant wealth. In other words, power to gain wealth to establish this covenant here and in the nations of the earth. What a time to invest. What a time to receive fresh oil! What a time to step into this burning lamp awakening.

God wants you to receive a perpetual flow of provision. But to keep your pipeline flowing, you must give so you can receive. "Give, and it shall be given unto you, pressed down, shaken together and running over shall men pour into your bosom," Jesus admonished (Luke 6:38).

Regarding tithes and offerings, God challenged us to "test Me now in this," says the Lord of hosts, "if I will not open for you the windows of heaven and pour out for you a blessing until it overflows. Then I will rebuke the devourer for you, so that it will not destroy the fruits of the ground; nor will your vine in the field cast its grapes," says the Lord of hosts" (Malachi 3:10-12).

An open heaven for the oil to flow. The devourer rebuked. Though the years we have personally received many incredible testimonies of donors who experienced major breakthrough after sowing into Lamplighter. That's the Kingdom way!

Not by might nor power, but by My Spirit, says the Lord. What a promise to your for your new season.

CHAPTER FOUR
Conflict of Thrones

The midnight cry is a summons to a wedding. Behold the Bridegroom! He's coming. Rise up to meet Him! But it's important to note this summons is issued at a midnight hour of history, defined by a midnight crisis.

In this chapter we're going to explore the biblical roots of this emerging crisis. We're going to identify geopolitical conflicts which will figure prominently from 2018-2020. Finally, now through the following chapter we're going to examine the midnight crisis in America surrounding the 2016 elections, as well as the extraordinary turnaround the Lord has granted.

Lets begin with a dream which warned of a midnight crisis regarding Iran. It was through this dream the Lord defined the crisis as a "Conflict of Thrones."

Washington's Midnight Wave

On July 13, 2015, a day before the Iranian Nuclear accords were announced, I saw Washington DC on the edge of a giant precipice. It was about to be flooded by a midnight wave. I immediately posted the dream for our Lamplighter readers.

In the dream this morning, I saw Washington DC from a different vantage point. Our Nation's Capitol was behind a gigantic cliff next to the ocean. The cliff was on the highest hill, and acted as an impenetrable barrier against the ocean's highest waves. Most of the city was built either on the hill towards the cliff, or below the hill in a valley.

Usually the ocean waves were at the base of the cliff, hundreds of feet below. But this time the ocean was actually close to cresting over the cliff—like a tsunami!

It was midnight—allegorically, when Paul Revere began his midnight ride. I had just left a group of young prayer warriors who had gathered in the city for their annual ministry time at David's Tent. I immediately drove back to the crowded homes of the young prayer warriors I had visited. I felt I had to visit them personally so they would actually believe the warning and respond.

I shouted to them, FLOOD! Water cresting over the hill—a disaster never seen before!

As I glanced towards the hill, a little water began to flow over the bank. There was no traffic in the city, as everybody was asleep. No one was trying to escape, because nobody was even aware. Then I looked again and saw flood waters rushing down from the hill towards the street I was on. I stepped inside an open garage with a thick brick wall, hoping to lessen the impact of the coming torrent.

Again, while praying over this dream the Lord spoke to me the phrase, "Conflict of Thrones." Just a day later, Secretary John Kerry announced the Iranian nuclear accords on behalf of President Obama. As the deal was being sealed, Iranian leaders continued to threaten Israel and the United States. Ayatollah Khamenei even vowed that "Israel won't even exist in 25 years."

Congress was given 60 days to review the deal, voting in favor of the deal on September 10. At that very time, intercessors began to gather in Washington DC. My friend Jason Hershey launched the 24-7 David's Tent on 9-11 or September 11.

Amazingly, the Iranian deal released 150 billion dollars immediately into the Iranian economy, accelerating capacities to terrorize Israel and Sunni nations of the Mideast. Over decades Iran has been dedicated to igniting a Palestinian uprising or intifada. Terror groups such as Hezbollah and Hamas are being resourced towards this end.

Maybe it's not a coincidence that on, September 11, sudden violence surged on the Temple Mount. Tensions have remained at a heightened level ever since then, to this day.

Though I believe we dodged a bullet with the 2016 elections, the challenge remains a red alert. It's going to be very difficult to regain the ground we once had. Many have surmised that the window of opportunity to thwart Iran's worst intentions has already passed, and a terrible Mideast conflict may now be unavoidable.

Jesus Prophesies the Midnight Crisis

As recorded in Matthew 24, Jesus warned about wars and rumors of wars, earthquakes and famines, betrayals and false prophets, tribulations and martyrdom as characteristics of the birth pangs leading towards the end of the age. He also warned of the rise of lawlessness causing the love carried in the hearts of many to grow cold. This is hauntingly obvious in our world right now.

For a long time Jesus' prophetic statements puzzled me. Because in truth every generation has suffered from these same challenges. And suddenly I realized that's exactly the point. According to the Jewish worldview, history is cyclical not linear. Patterns repeat themselves, generally at a heightened level if left unchecked. And Jesus is saying that the crises already occurring will accelerate significantly as we move into history's midnight hour.

ACCORDING TO THE JEWISH WORLDVIEW, HISTORY IS CYCLICAL NOT LINEAR. PATTERNS REPEAT THEMSELVES, GENERALLY AT A HEIGHTENED LEVEL IF LEFT UNCHECKED

This principle is nowhere more apparent than in Christ's prophetic observation, "For nation will rise against nation, and kingdom against kingdom." Jesus extrapolated from the conflict of his day to prophesy an end-time conflict which would define the hour.

A conflict of thrones.

But the man who gave the prophecy is also the ultimate King over these kingdoms. And as we move towards this new season of history, we are going to see Jesus engaged in this "conflict of thrones" like no other time in history. This will eventually culminate when He confronts the ultimate expression of evil as He returns to the earth.

Thank God, Jesus is not waiting until the final hour of history to exercise His rulership over evil domains. We are in this season right now. Jesus' mother Mary, or Miriam, prophesied over our time of history when Christ was still in her womb. "He brings down rulers from their thrones!" (Luke 1:52).

Summit Vision: Moses Movement Globally Released!

In November 2017, Jolene and I participated in the Global Prophetic Summit, hosted by Cindy Jacobs around the 500th anniversary of the Protestant Reformation. Prophets from America and across the entire world were convened, perhaps for the first time in recorded history.

During the gathering the Lord showed me two visions conveying His real-time work in nations. The first vision occurred just as a private global roundtable began. I shared prophetically:

I see a glorious procession of angelic hosts from all the nations entering into Heaven's council. These angelic hosts are being honored and celebrated, much as we celebrate each other here. Heaven's council has now been convened in synergy with this global council of prophets. As Heaven and earth join together, we are entering a defining moment. HISTORY WILL LITERALLY BE MADE.

What transpired later in the meeting was nothing less than astounding. A leader from Zimbabwe stood with tears in his eyes, asking for prayer for his nation and for Africa. Joseph Garlington, an African American leader, wept and prayed by his side. Soon the stage was rushed by leaders from every continent, many in travailing prayer for breakthrough.

We prayed during this time that Zimbabwe's cruel dictator Robert Mugabe would be removed from office. It stunned us to hear news reports later in the evening. Because just after we prayed, Zimbabwe's army moved into the capital and placed Mugabe under house arrest!

Within a week he was deposed from office, and another leader assumed the presidency.

(He brings rulers down from their thrones.) This happened in real-time. Amazingly, years beforehand Cindy Jacobs had actually seen Mugabe's downfall and prophesied this very moment. How the Lord orchestrates His prophetic history is simply profound.

As the Global Prophetic Summit drew to a close, I saw another vision which correlated to the first one. Heaven's council concluded in an incredible way. I saw the angelic hosts standing on top of the summit of a huge mountain, with pathways on all sides connecting to each continent. Each were being launched from the mountain of His council to return to their respective nations. They were being commissioned to work with leaders from each nation, much as the Angel of the Lord worked with Moses. Preparing the way for a freedom procession as promised in Exodus 23:20.

I knew the histories of nations were again being defined. Governmentally from God's Throne, a new move of God was being released. (A global Moses movement to counter a global pharaoh movement holding His covenant people captive.)

> I KNEW THE HISTORIES OF NATIONS WERE AGAIN BEING DEFINED. GOVERNMENTALLY FROM GOD'S THRONE, A REVOLUTIONARY NEW MOVE WAS BEING RELEASED. A GLOBAL MOSES MOVEMENT

Then came the launch. I looked down one of the pathways and saw it was a winter Olympic ski jump. A skier in a white ski suit, which I knew was an angel, lunged down the path towards the jump. The acceleration was tremendous. A tremendous recovery of momentum!

But as I followed this angel down the slope, I realized the cost of obtaining this movement and its benefits. It required making a giant leap of faith!

Friends, it's time to embrace this new Moses movement. It's time to accelerate and leap into His purposes for nations. Watch how the Lord opens the opportunity for you to synergize with His angelic hosts to advance His purposes in your sphere. Watch how you begin to soar over the obstacles which once constrained you!

As the Global Prophetic Summit drew to a close, Cindy Jacobs led the crowd in praying over the tense situation between North Korea and South Korea. Freedom! During this time, the unction came on me to governmentally declare the release of this Moses movement I had seen. LET MY PEOPLE GO!

When I returned to my seat, I wondered if there was more to the imagery of the downhill ski jumper than I first perceived. Looking up "winter Olympics" on Google took my breath away. Because in 2018, the winter Olympics are being held in South Korea!

What is God saying? On a global level, a new "Moses movement" is being released to turn the tide of this "conflict of thrones" in which many nations are engaged. Watch how the conflict defining the Koreas begins to shift even beginning in the winter of 2018.

Further, I believe this global movement is poised to reverberate in the nations with the same magnitude as the Protestant Reformation. It could even define the reformation of this hour. The Lord is thundering from the mountain summit, Let My people go!

Conflict of Thrones 2018-2020

Lets briefly examine a eight major conflicts which will figure prominently now through 2020. Two have been explored already, but it is helpful to summarize for perspective.

1. *The Korea Conflict*—As mentioned, tensions are high and America's commitment remains resolute that there will be no toleration of a nuclear-capable North Korea. We must settle this conflict first in the heavenlies. He brings down rulers from their thrones! But the dangers of a nuclear Korea intensify greatly as we examine the nation's alliance with Iran.

2. *The Shia-Sunni Conflict*—Iran is the primary representative of Shia Islam. As Benjamin Netanyahu pointed out in his renegade address to Congress, Iran is actually a greater threat to Sunni nations in the Mideast than to Israel. This is especially true with Saudi Arabia, host of Mecca and Medina, Islam's holiest cities. Iran's recent aggression is now being countered by an historic

alliance between Saudi Arabia, Egypt, Jordan, Israel and the United States. Watch how covert aggression becomes open conflict in the days ahead. Eventually the Lord will turn this for good, even for the emergence of the Isaiah 19 highway.

3. *The Israel-Palestinian Conflict*—With this emerging alliance comes increased pressure for a "land for peace agreement" between Israel and the Palestinians. An American proposal for a two-state solution is due in January 2018. The warning remains from God regarding His covenant land—do not divide Israel, and do not divide Jerusalem! (Joel 3:2). I believe our supernatural enemy seeks an escalation of war between the two entities. Stopping the bloodshed could provide a great excuse for a dramatic intervention by globalists—perhaps the UN—to take over Jerusalem from both Israel and the Palestinians, and declare it an international city for global governance.

4. *The Temple Mount Conflict*—The ultimate conflict of thrones defining the end of days concerns the Temple Mount. But much of our conflict even today concerns this mountain God claims as His own throne.

5. *Nationalism vs Globalism*—This issue became the driving force of the 2016 elections as President Trump campaigned to "Make America great again." Before addressing this conflict I first want to clearly differentiate between global engagement, which is mandated by the Lord, and the movement of global elites tied to idolatry, seeking to bring nations into subjugation. And as pictured in the Book of Revelation, globalism actually ushers in the ultimate "conflict of thrones." Always remember it is ultimately a spiritual conflict first.

6. *The Political Spirit*—Canadian leader Faisal Malick wrote a book which is so vital for our time. *The Political Spirit* Leaders in the body of Christ must discern from the Lord about the true intentions of our political leaders from state to state and

nationally. Not all who name the Name of Jesus are yielded to His intentions in their agendas. Herod declared an intention to worship Israel's newborn King even while planning a campaign to kill him. Keep your eyes open.

7. **Deep State Deliverance**—Soon after Trump's election, a few high-level government leaders pursued covert sabotage to usurp the new leader and restore their hidden agendas. Their treasonous efforts included countless security breaches, illegal leaks to media, etc. They became known as "the Deep State." And God is saying, Let there be light. As with Genesis 1, a deep state deliverance.

8. **America's Mid-term Elections & 2020 Presidential Elections**— Evangelicals pushed President Trump across the threshold in 2016, and into a new season of reformation. But many simply went back to sleep. A huge question is whether the momentum of this turnaround will be sustained. It's really up to us. First in prayer, and then with action. We must have 2020 vision!

The Abomination of Desolation

In Matthew 25, Jesus warned about "the abomination of desolation which was spoken of through Daniel the prophet, standing in the holy place" (Matt. 24:7). There's such confusion surrounding this passage. But as we gain clarity, we can see how our world today is already being impacted by the very abomination Jesus warned about. Further, like Moses we can gain strategy to catalyze revolutionary change.

Ultimately Jesus is warning about a supremely evil figure, a grand master of idolatry and the occult, who will in time set up a global throne of rulership on the Temple Mount in Jerusalem, Israel.

That's the abomination part. According to the Bible, he's going to be a lot like Antiochus IV Epiphanes, who dedicated the Jewish Temple to Zeus and Baal and made unholy sacrifices to seal his demonic covenant. He's also going to be a lot like Adolf Hitler in both his global pursuit of power and his resolve to exterminate God's covenant people from the earth.

What is this abomination? Idolatry. The end-time pharaoh Jesus prophesied about is merely a stronger manifestation of the very same evil destroying lives even now.

> "And every spirit that does not confess Jesus is not from God; this is the spirit of the antichrist, of which you have heard that it is coming, and now it is already in the world" (1 John 4:3).

Plain and simple, the abomination of idolatry causes desolation. Especially when this idolatry is embraced by God's own people. It's an antichrist spirit.

The story of Hosea's bride puts a human face this terrible evil experienced by multitudes. Further, like no other prophet Hosea conveys his revelation in terms of bridal imagery. Hosea represents the Bridegroom whom he serves, Israel's own Messiah. And his bride represents Israel, His covenant people.

The only problem is that the bride to whom he is devoted has compromised herself with another lover.

Not getting enough pleasure, power, provision or influence through your Jesus? Try a sample of this. Pretty good, right? Yeah and I have so much more where that came from! Just bow your knee to me, and all this can be yours...

That's how Hosea's bride was seduced. Hosea lavished His covenant affections on her. But she still fell for the promises of Baal—more pleasure, more affection, more gain and self-fulfillment at the expense of others. She soon found out that the very pleasures she thought would free her actually made her a slave.

Not a coincidence that the name "Baal" means both "husband" and "taskmaster." This begs the question. What's your baal? What has mastery over you outside of Jesus? Can your loyalty be bought or sold? At what price?

And how long are you going to tolerate Baal's captivity over your life?

Satan understands that, when God's covenant people become seduced by idolatry, it causes the ultimate defilement of the covenant relationship Jesus has devoted His life to secure. No wonder idolatry is the abomination which causes desolation. It strikes at the very heart of the Bridegroom who died to redeem us all.

Desolation

Seeing the extraordinary importance Jesus Himself placed upon this subject, why doesn't the issue of idolatry gain more press from pulpits today? Why are so few warning about the negative consequences? It remains puzzling how countless churches and houses of prayer, seemingly devoted to Jesus, still tolerate what He passionately deplores. There can be no compromise with idolatry, no fellowship between Christ and Baal.

Many are suffering needlessly as a result. Many are actually experiencing desolation in their temple, the holy place of their own hearts.

Scripture is very clear. Those who practice idolatry or occult activity are opening themselves and their generational line to a curse. Idolatry always ultimately releases torment, rejection, sexual deviation, financial hardship and subjugation.

This is best pictured by a prophetic experience given to the prophet Ezekiel. He was taken in a vision to an idol which had been erected at the north gate of God's Temple. Once again, this is not a symbolic expression but a literal Temple on the literal Temple Mount in Jerusalem. Needless to say, the "idol which provokes to jealousy, standing at the north gate" was the exact antithesis of God's command as a Bridegroom to His covenant people. "You shall have no other gods before me!"

What the Lord conveyed to His friend is very telling. "Son of man, do you see what they are doing, the great abominations which the house of Israel are committing here, so that I would be far from My sanctuary?" (Ezekiel 8:6).

God's judgement soon followed. The Lord lifted His glory, the presence and power of His Spirit, from the land. And His own people were sent into captivity in Babylon.

The abomination of idolatry causes desolation. Hosea's bride is cast into the wilderness. God's people are sent into exile. The land mourns. This principle is as sure as gravity.

Note that this antichrist spirit is continually seeking thrones of influence, especially governmental thrones. But again, the throne of your own heart is what he covets the most—especially if you are a follower of God.

The Political Spirit

We all know there seems to be an undercurrent of spiritual oppression surrounding politics. Every wonder why? Lets take a brief look at what our friend Faisal Malick calls "the political spirit."

One warning Faisal gave is particularly applicable today. "The political spirit will always try to buy, corrupt, or manipulate prophets in this manner to suit its hidden agenda" (The Political Spirit, pg. 79). The stakes are so high today. And that's all the more reason to keep humble before the Throne and seek His ways and His discernment.

It's important to understand that when Satan tempted Jesus, it was primarily as a political ruler. And he had a hidden agenda in mind. The enemy had no grid to understand how Israel's King was going to lay down His own life to redeem mankind. All he knew—or thought he knew—were prophetic scriptures which referenced Israel's Messiah as the king of the world. In his mind, a political ruler.

Scripture makes this clear. "None of the rulers of this world understood it. If they had, they would not have crucified the Lord of glory" (1 Corinthians 2:8, NCV).

Satan took Jesus to a summit, and showed Him all the kingdoms of the world and their glory (see Matthew 4:8-11). He actually had the audacity to ask Israel's Messiah to worship him, promoting himself as the conduit to Jesus' prophetic destiny. "All this will be yours," he intoned, "if you bow down and worship me."

The throne of the entire world. A shortcut to receiving His kingship which completely avoided the sacrifice of the cross. Note that this experience would not have been classified as a temptation unless there was actual substance to it.

Thank God, Jesus replied with great clarity. We should do the same. "Go, Satan! For it is written, You shall worship the Lord your God only, and serve Him only!"

What's conveyed here remains the primary way we are tempted into compromise with the enemy—especially governmental leaders. The ends justify the means. Everybody compromises. Just shift your alignment, nobody has to know.

Bow your knees to me, and all this can be yours.

Beloved, your worship conveys your covenant. Really, your worship seals your covenant. And your covenants establish your thrones of authority. That's ultimately what the enemy is after.

Thrones behind the Thrones

Pharaoh in Egypt is a great example of this. Remember Pharaoh set up his throne of rulership as a literal portal to the demonic realm. As part of his "swearing in," he literally invoked demonic principalities from the spiritual realm to rule with him and through him.

The Bible clearly warns that in the end of days, an evil ruler will set up his throne of rulership in like manner. Through this he will literally become the embodiment of satanic power in the earth. A modern Pharaoh. The ultimate "abomination of desolation."

That said, you can see how thrones of rulership have become compromised by ties to idolatry through these covenants of compromise even today.

You could say that through his temptation of Jesus, the enemy was attempting to establish a literal "shadow government" over Israel. A "deep state" dominion. A throne in the spiritual realm that accessed and released demonic rulership through the thrones of earth.

In short, a throne behind the throne.

These occult thrones were at the very pinnacle of Nazi power, and they continue to empower many dictators today. At the core they all connect thrones of influence or authority to the demonic realm.

What can be done? We'll explore this more in the next chapter. But remember the Maccabees. They renewed their desolate heritage by restoring covenant with God, divorced from idolatry—and thereby launched a new beginning for their land.

America's Midnight Crisis

As with Israel, America was founded at its inception by covenant with the Lord. The year 2020 will actually mark the 400th anniversary of the signing of the Mayflower Compact. Written in the Presence of the Lord by their own testimony, the Pilgrims committed what became our land and government to "the glory of God and the advancement of the Christian faith." Many other Christian communities also established their spheres in the new world by similar covenants with Him.

But these covenantal foundations soon became intentionally compromised and defiled. As our book Crown & Throne conveys, secret societies such as Freemasonry brought tremendous mixture into every aspect of our culture, including the governmental world. Unitarianism adopted a primary tenet of Freemasonry—that all religions form an altar to "god" or a pathway to the "divine"—no matter whether the religion of choice is Islam, Hinduism, Buddhism, Witchcraft, or outright Satanism.

Soon the embrace of all forms of idolatry became a religion unto itself. Like ancient Israel, America quite literally loved the Lord but served the Baals (II Kings 17:41). But there are always consequences. Remember—the abomination of idolatry causes desolation.

As America became the leader of the free world, we also led the world into choosing darkness. After Israel was reborn, former presidents and leaders empowered Freemasonry and other occult expressions of global governance in God's covenant land. The sexual revolution unleashed promiscuity, pornography, sexual abuse, no-cause divorce and even sex trafficking in our land at a magnitude unimaginable to our forefathers. We soon saw the legalization not only of abortion, but even even late-term abortion. New age occult practices flourished. And even overt satanism spread like fire through our nation.

Beloved, in this conflict of thrones we are defined by what we tolerate.

And the stain of this sin has been on all our hands.

It's so important to note that through our history many presidents and governmental leaders have overtly bowed their knees to Baal. Many have been using their seats of authority for their personal gain at the expense of the American people. Some have even openly promoted sin and even forced through laws mandating a significant compromise of God's heart and standard.

That said, when the American people elected our 44th President, I'm not sure we fully understood the change he envisioned to bring to our land. Because the governmental mandates forced upon the American people—to accept, embrace and propagate overt idolatry and sin—was never part of the equation.

It grieves me to write this. I actually prayed more for President Obama than any president in my lifetime. With all my heart, I wanted our nation's first black president to carry the torch of Lincoln and King and through Jesus' power become an historic catalyst of genuine freedom for our nation and world.

From my perspective, he chose a much different path.

And again, as we examine some of the challenges brought on by the Obama administration, we clearly see how many tracks were laid over decades, even centuries beforehand.

That said, it was quite a shock when former President Obama launched his historic presidency by traveling to Egypt and announcing that America was no longer a Christian nation. Soon after, a war was waged against virtually every remnant of Judeo-Christian values still embraced by our culture.

Nativity scenes were banned in the public square. Public prayer in the name of Jesus became restricted, for military services and even high school football games. The Internal Revenue Service was directed to impede and scrutinize conservative groups and even Christian ministries—including the Billy Graham Evangelistic Association. Marriage actually became governmentally redefined, shifting the institution from the biblical standard for the first time in perhaps 6,000 years.

It seemed like every moral boundary sourced in a Judeo-Christian worldview was suddenly under attack. Yet the assault was not only on our moral boundaries, but the constitutional boundaries of our Nation as well.

By presidential mandate, our own borders became largely undefended and unsecured. International trade pacts actually yielded the sovereignty of our nation to global governance. The constitutional boundaries defining the balance of power even became breached.

Further, the terror group ISIS was allowed to run free across the undefended borders of Iraq. This after US soldiers had just sacrificed life and limb to secure these same borders. More than 4,000 US service-men and service-women died. As many as 600,000 were injured in defense of Iraq. To simply turn the nation over to ISIS was in my opinion indefensible.

Then there was the Iran deal. In my opinion, a travesty which again put not only Israel and America in jeopardy, but all the Sunni Muslim nations of the Mideast.

As a final defining moment, Obama actually closed his presidency by pursuing a quest similar to that of Antiochus IV Epiphanes regarding the Temple Mount. The only remnant of the structure still intact from the Jewish Temple period is the Western Wall. It is now, of course, the holiest site in all Judaism.

Amazingly, the President pushed through a last-minute UN resolution declaring the Western Wall to be "Palestinian land illegally occupied by Israel." In the spirit of Antiochus, he even accomplished this feat on December 23. Just two days before Christmas, and one day before the start of Hanukkah.

You can't make this stuff up. I'm serious. I say this through tears.

Through these missteps, America became thrust into a midnight crisis where our very identity as a freedom nation was at stake. Even more chilling was the fact that Hillary Clinton, his chosen successor, was poised to perpetuate and even greatly expand these same globalist policies, tied to idolatry and corruption.

Thank God the Christian community gained resolve to stand against

Clinton's campaign and the corruption, which was every day being exposed. Only now, as sexual abuse by powerbrokers from both right and left are being exposed, are Democratic party members admitting that it was abhorrent to overlook and even justify the many indiscretions of our former President and his wife.

I am reminded of the vineyard owner Naboth, who was confronted by Jezebel when she and Ahab wanted to claim his land. "God forbid," Naboth replied, "that I should give you the inheritance of my forefathers" (1 Kings 21:3).

That said, over many years it became obvious that politics alone could in no way save our nation. Instead, Heaven's intervention was needed. And to authentically secure this intervention, our broken covenant needed to be restored.

LET MY PEOPLE GO.

CHAPTER FIVE
The Midnight Turnaround

In October of 2007 I had a dream which conveyed both the season we were entering into, and the sustenance which would keep and preserve us through a coming midnight hour.

In this dream, the mountains of Colorado Springs framed a vast forest of evergreens, cascading down from the ridge I was on. Pikes Peak was snow-capped and towered over the highest summits of the front range. All was bright and brilliant.

I was seated with prophetic leader Dutch Sheets at a large table. Its soft white hue was shining from a sun unshielded by any clouds.

Dutch suddenly got up from the table and left. Immediately the bright sky began to darken, as if controlled by a remote dimmer switch. Colors faded, then disappeared. The mountains, even Pikes Peak, became indistinguishable from the sky. I could not even see my hand in front of my face. All went completely dark.

All, that is, except for the table. It remained luminous. The only creation of God or man to remain unconquered by the encroaching darkness.

Suddenly Dutch reappeared. This time he sat down at the head of the table. I asked him, "What is the Lord speaking to you?" And he replied, "This year God is granting apostolic authority to release the river of God and direct its path."

When I awoke, I immediately knew four things. First, through the dream the Lord was clearly communicating that we were approaching a midnight hour for our nation. And the only thing which will remain luminous is the Table of the Lord. Communion. Covenant. Jesus' own body and blood, given for the remission of our sins and the healing of our bodies. The only evidence before Heaven's Court which completely justifies us.

By darkened night or shining day, the Table of the Lord remains our only source of light and spiritual strength.

I also knew that Dutch represented a prototype of the forerunner ministry. Through this dream the Lord was conveying the re-emergence of a forerunner spirit or forerunner anointing. I didn't realize then that the Lord had embedded a literal timetable within the dream. Dutch and his family literally moved from Colorado Springs in 2008, and then returned in 2015.

From this prophetic dream, I also knew that in the midst of America's midnight hour, authority from Heaven would be granted to release a force—a current—powerful enough to turn the tide of our nation.

The Presidential elections of 2016 marked this turning point.

2016 Election Turnaround

The stakes were so high. I'll never forget when, in the summer of 2015, Holy Spirit spoke that we only had a limited window of opportunity to catalyze national turnaround. It was clear that we could either get back on track or continue a downward spiral towards global governance, idolatry and corruption to the extent that God's dream for our land could actually have been beyond recovery.

The election cycle was full of unforgettable events—especially when revolutionary business magnate Donald J. Trump appeared among the politicos. The moment I remember most was the night of November 8, when the election results began to pour in. Unexpectedly the momentum shifted towards Trump. We launched into midnight watch, with the unfolding drama and commentary from the news channels keeping us breathless through the early morning hours.

And through the midnight watch we saw a literal "midnight turnaround." Perhaps the most dramatic electoral shift in decades, if not in American history.

For two years straight, "turnaround" was the literal language God had given us to pray over the election. Specifically He had released a "turnaround verdict" from Heaven's Court. And I want to make something very clear. This turnaround wasn't catalyzed by politics, it was catalyzed by Jesus in response to extraordinary prayer and even an unprecedented covenant rededication. And because of this, the political world doesn't technically own the turnaround. God does—and so do we, as the body of Christ.

Remember—separation and rededication can launch a new beginning. If He can do it in the government of America, He can absolutely do it in whatever sphere you are impacting as well. We were inspired by the Maccabees that, by reconsecrating the ruins of our desolate heritage to the Lord, divorced from our historic idolatry, we too could receive a new beginning from His hand. This was the only sure foundation we could depend upon for the turnaround we hoped against hope to receive.

And against all odds, we have received this turnaround. At least the beginning of one.

Divorcing Baal

Keep in mind I had walked through a personal crisis in which ties had to be severed to release a new beginning for myself and my children. So I immediately resonated with a cry from Dutch Sheets and others that our nation needed to receive a divorce from Baal—in other words, from our historic idolatry. Dutch taught that Baal was the strongman over our nation. To secure the destiny of our nation, we needed to divorce Baal and remarry Jesus. It was haunting how this mirrored my own journey.

On July 7, 2007 Dutch Sheets, Lou Engle and James Goll gathered tens of thousands of people for the Call Nashville, with a singular focus on divorcing Baal. In Hebrew, seven connotes covenant. And on 07-07-07 amazing prayers were prayed and tremendous vision cast as we sought to repair America's covenant with God. We had high expectation for change.

The only problem: things didn't turn for the better. In fact they seemed to only get worse.

I realize now that the Call Nashville was actually God's marriage proposal for America, not the final verdict. Heaven's court needed to be fully satisfied for this divorce from Baal and reconsecration to Jesus to be rendered valid. And a few missing pieces to this equation soon came to the forefront.

First, marriage is a legally binding contract. And for a marriage to be annulled, it's not enough to simply declare intention. A legal case must be made, and a court must actually rule to grant the divorce. The Court of Heaven being the governing body in this case, of course.

> MARRIAGE IS A LEGALLY BINDING CONTRACT. AND FOR A MARRIAGE TO BE ANNULLED, IT'S NOT ENOUGH SIMPLY TO DECLARE INTENTION. A LEGAL CASE MUST BE MADE, AND A COURT MUST ACTUALLY RULE

And the issue of present and generational idolatry was mandated by Heaven's Court to be addressed at a magnitude that was far more comprehensive than we had ever imagined.

Most Comprehensive Repudiation of Idolatry in US History

Late in 2008, Iowa prophet Katherine Watsey gave the following prophetic word to apostle John Benefiel, director of the Heartland Apostolic Prayer Network, and prophet Cindy Jacobs, director of the Reformation Prayer Network. Note that I'm summarizing the word. "You must divorce Baal at all lodges, mosques, abortion clinics and other altars of idolatry in the nation," she declared. "This is necessary to 'knock the legs out' from under the elites who are trying to claim control over our land. And God will respond by restoring his glory and sending his third great awakening!"

All altars of historic and present idolatry needed to be prayed over onsite across the nation, seeking the divorce from Baal. Then the verdict would be granted.

What followed was the largest and most comprehensive repudiation of idolatry in American history. Thank God the prayer movement actually mobilized. Led by John Benefiel and Cindy Jacobs, more than 10,000 altars of idolatry were prayed over in every small village and large metropolis of every state in the nation. In 2013 we were also directed to pray over every abortion clinic in the nation. Seeking the Lord to grant a divorce from our historic sin-empowered idolatry, restore covenant with us, and grant us a new beginning.

How did God respond? Just like He promised.

Covenant Restored

The project to divorce Baal was largely culminated on July 4, 2011. Jolene and I were privileged to host a team of apostolic leaders from across the nation, including Apostle Benefiel, Negiel Bigpond, Bishop Harry Jackson and many others. The quest to pray onsite at these 10,000 altars had largely been completed. Further, Apostle John had just completed his personal assignment to visit every state and governmentally pray through the divorce decree from Baal.

We gathered on the steps of the Lincoln Memorial, facing the Washington Monument, and presented the largely completed work to the Lord. We then presented Him with a Declaration of Covenant, asking Him to marry the land again according to the covenants of our forefathers.

Our final request before the Throne was that a sign would be granted that He had heard us, and renewed covenant with our land. Rick Ridings, the founder of the 24-7 Succat Hallel in Jerusalem, had seen a vision of a giant nutcracker sent by God to crack the hard shell of demonic resistance over Washington DC.

This resistance was being clearly addressed through the project to divorce Baal. So we simply asked, "Grant us a divorce from Baal! Grant us a renewal of covenant! And as a sign that You have heard us… Crack that nut!"

On August 23, 2011—50 days to the day of our plea—Washington DC was rocked by a giant earthquake. Gargoyles toppled from the

National Cathedral. And the Washington Monument quite literally cracked. We knew the sign of our covenant restoration had been given. The demands of Heaven's Court thus satisfied, His verdict had been granted.

More signs followed. Here are two stunning expressions set to redefine culture in Washington DC.

Within a year of the covenant rededication, my friend Jason Hershey launched a pioneering project to bring 24-7 worship on the National Mall, beginning with the White House Ellipse! Davids Tent today is actually welcoming the Lord into Washington DC 24-7-365!

And within the very same year, Hobby Lobby founder Steve Green decided to establish a Museum of the Bible. I heard that he first looked at major cities in the Bible Belt for a location. But he actually decided on Washington DC!

We saw covenant with Christ restored. And all of the sudden God gifted Washington DC with a national Ark of the Covenant—a witness to His covenant goodness to our land, to Israel, and to the nations!

You can't make this up. Remember, separation and dedication releases a new beginning. And the largest and most comprehensive repudiation of idolatry in American history soon became the legal foundation for the largest and most comprehensive governmental turnaround in American history.

> THE LARGEST AND MOST COMPREHENSIVE REPUDIATION OF IDOLATRY IN AMERICAN HISTORY SOON BECAME THE LEGAL FOUNDATION FOR THE LARGEST AND MOST COMPREHENSIVE REPUDIATION OF IDOLATRY IN AMERICAN HISTORY.

Revolution—Securing the Legal Foundation

"We, therefore, the Representatives of the united States of America, in General Congress, Assembled, APPEALING TO THE SUPREME JUDGE OF THE WORLD for the rectitude of our intentions…"

Did you know that our founders actually appealed to the Court of Heaven—and even to the Supreme Judge? This legal language actually became the pivot point for the entire Declaration of Independence as the American Revolution was declared.

Our founders petitioned Heaven to receive the legal foundation for their Revolution. And in our day, we knew we had to approach the same bench to receive a verdict that would launch God's intended governmental turnaround. Like the Maccabees and the colonists, it was indeed a revolution.

Faneuil Hall — Continental Congress

In 2014 the Lord brought forth a very clear summons. "Gather on 7-22 at Faneuil Hall Boston, because on 7-22 I am releasing My Daniel 7:22 judgement in favor of the saints."

Faneuil Hall is known as the "womb of the Revolution" because it was a primary gathering place for Boston's revolutionaries. Within its sacred walls, growing outrage soon became a united outcry. Raucous debates compelled a small band of farmers, tradesmen, rulers and writers to make a courageous stand for freedom. Even pastors turned revolutionaries—and soon shaped the course of history.

Oh, that we would all be so persuaded today.

Anyway, when God spoke, I immediately saw how Faneuil Hall would make an incredible venue to receive this Throne Room verdict. It was the perfect venue to convene a Continental Congress and together receive the Daniel 7:22 judgement we are now calling the "turnaround verdict."

From Outrage to Outcry

We also knew that, to see a revolutionary turnaround in our time, America's latent outrage needed to be shifted into a resounding outcry against the overarching influence subjugating our land and culture. That's what happened during the days of the Revolution. A midnight cry was released collectively as well as through Paul Revere.

Outrage to outcry. Little did I know that this united outcry would soon become the driving force behind the 2016 elections. Here's a bit of free advice. As we move forward we must do the same.

The Turnaround Verdict

Lets take a brief glimpse into Daniel's vision of the Turnaround

Verdict, beginning with verse 21:

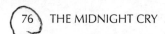

> (21) I kept watching, and that horn was waging war with the saints and overpowering them

> (22) Until the Ancient of Days came, and judgment was rendered in favor of the saints of the Highest One, and the time arrived when the saints took possession of the kingdom.

Until this verdict was released, the Bible says that the saints of God were being overpowered by a demonic horn, a symbol of an antichrist spirit. Theologians have long debated whether this antichrist horn represents a spiritual entity or a human being. I personally believe both! This antichrist horn is a human being who, like Pharaoh of old, is empowered in life and governance by a high-level demonic power. United together in covenant for evil.

The Bible implies that, at the time of this decision, the saints were doing everything they knew to do—worshiping, fasting, praying, tithing, assembling together, living righteous lives in their professions and at home. They were mobilizing to affect the seven mountains of society for God.

Yet instead of victory, they were losing ground at every turn! Isolated, divided, marginalized, impoverished, defrauded of covenant promises. Many even making the ultimate sacrifice, the flame of their very lives extinguished for their faith.

Sounds familiar, doesn't it? Way too familiar.

That's when the Court of Heaven intervenes and rules in their favor. The Beast that opposed them is immediately restrained. And in every dimension of life and the spirit where the saints were opposed, they suddenly win! These same war-weary believers are immediately released to possess the Kingdom.

It's for this reason we call this judicial decision "the turnaround verdict."

Please note that a Courtroom verdict accomplishes for the saints what their own spiritual warfare and societal engagement could not alone attain. As you will see, the Lord Himself honors, upholds and defends every verdict that He legitimately renders. Revelation 19:11 describes how He judges, or renders a verdict, and then wages war to establish this verdict in the earth.

So for the saints, it's simply a matter of time.

I want to emphasize again that the legal foundation for the governmental turnaround we were pursuing was actually established through the divorcement of Baal and restoration of covenant with Christ. We were about to see this verdict established at an unprecedented level. And the "turnaround verdict" gave a clear description of what to expect. Judgement in favor of the saints, restraining the darkness, releasing the saints to possess the Kingdom.

2014—First Election Turnaround

The first clear evidence of turnaround occurred as America's 2014 elections shifted dramatically. At the Faneuil Hall gathering, Chuck Pierce prophesied a 100 day watch to see this verdict brought to bear upon our nation. As we counted the days, the 100th day was very close to election day.

Needless to say we kept vigil in Washington DC and, with our Lamplighter family, from Washington to Washington over these 100 days. What followed was unprecedented. American voters soon unleashed one of the most historic Congressional turnarounds in history, as well as a historic state by state turnaround in respective governors' races.

2015—Israel's Election Turnaround

Then in 2015 the Lord assigned us to pray for Israel's election over the final 10 days in Jerusalem. I can only provide an overview of this for now. God showed us clearly that He desired Prime Minister Netanyahu to win. But nobody in either Israel or America actually thought this was possible due to extraordinary pressure from the US.

Remember, Netanyahu stood against the Iranian nuclear deal during a special joint session of Congress just before his own election. This drew the ire of President Obama, who put tremendous pressure on the Israeli people to remove him. Obama's top campaign manager was even sent to Israel to work for Netanyahu's opposition. And it's come out now that State Department funds were channeled to help fund his opponent!

When we got to Israel, we discovered that most everyone wanted Prime Minister Netanyahu to retain his seat. But again, nobody thought this was possible—not even the intercessors! As we ministered in Jerusalem, Jolene and I immediately began by repenting for the pride of Washington DC in assuming a right to rule God's covenant land. We shared, prayed and decreed with a focus on Daniel 7:22, God's turnaround verdict.

Judgement in favor of the saints. Restraining the beast. Releasing the saints to possess the Kingdom!

On Israel's election day we literally became watchmen on the walls. A friend commissioned us. We then walked the walls of Jerusalem towards the Western Wall. And as we walked, Holy Spirit thundered to me the following: "As you have stood for My elections in My covenant land, so I will stand for a turnaround in your presidential election in 2016!"

Note that at the time Holy Spirit spoke, nobody believed Netanyahu would win. But against all odds, later that night he did. Turnaround.

2016—Presidential Election and the Turnaround Tour

With a promise from Jesus while literally watching on the walls of Jerusalem, Jolene and I were thrust into the 2016 elections with incredible hope for God's intended turnaround. Daniel 7:22 again came into focus.

We actually traveled to all 50 states over seven months on a revival journey called the "Glory Train-Turnaround Tour," prophesying and declaring the shift the Lord intended as we circled the entire nation by train. We carried with us the clear understanding that this scripture was validated by Heaven's Court through the divorcement from Baal and restoration of covenant with Jesus Christ. His authority was now being released to get us back on track.

And against all odds, we soon saw together the greatest governmental turnaround in modern history. It was amazing how the Lord led us to prophesy from state to state. Here are four highlights:

1. *Wisconsin, the Conductor State*—On Election Day, Wisconsin became the state that put Trump over the top. The Lord spoke to us on April 20 that Wisconsin was the "conductor state" which would either direct America down the right tracks or the wrong tracks.

2. *Pennsylvania, the Turnaround Womb*—Pennsylvania's turnaround secured Trump's victory. On Tuesday, April 22, Jolene prophesied in Pittsburgh that Pennsylvania was God's "Turnaround Womb." She saw the hand of the Lord come to a womb with a breached baby and turn the baby around. Later in Philadelphia, she saw how the baby was now "crowned" for birth. We were led to prophesy a "new birth of freedom!"

3. *Trump Turnaround*—Very unexpectedly, our Glory Train tour was routed through the Trump Towers in NYC. A friend from Washington DC had been hired by the Trump campaign in NYC. After the damaging tapes had been released she called and asked us to come pray onsite at Trump's campaign headquarters. We prayed Daniel 7:22, God's turnaround verdict. The timing was absolutely unmistakable. Our friend soon texted, "It all shifted from the week you came—literally." What an honor! "The Ancient of Days took His seat, and judgement was rendered in favor of the saints, and the time came fore the saints to possess the Kingdom" (Daniel 7:22).

4. *The Michigan Mantle*—Finally, Michigan became the 50th state and last stop of our 2016 Glory Train-Turnaround Tour. We finished a day before the election in the very state where an African American bishop had mantled Donald Trump with a Jewish prayer shawl earlier in the year. When I saw the photo,

the Lord spoke to me, "Never forget that Donald Trump was mantled for the presidency by an African American pastor from Detroit." Amazingly, even Michigan turned. And the pastor who mantled him even delivered the closing prayer at President Trump's inauguration!

I could share so much more. Suffice to say, the hand of the Lord was intricately involved in every facet of the revolutionary turnaround now shaking America and the nations. And the election victory of 2016 is simply a first fruit of God's work.

The Turnaround—Current Results

As I review this posting, it brings awe to my spirit to see how accurately the Lord conveyed to us, and to many prophets, the events which now define our world. There's a reason for it. We must remember that the political world did not birth the turnaround, God did. And therefore political leaders cannot take it away.

Below is a list of just a few of the extraordinary turnarounds we have seen since the Trump administration came into office.

1. *Israel Alliance Restored*—Remember President Obama's final defining act as president was to push through a UN resolution denying Israel's sovereignty over the Western Wall. One of President Trump's first priorities was to restore the diplomatic alliance between Israel and America and support God's covenant land once again. Including their right to national sovereignty.

2. *Economic Recovery*—Since Trump came to power, his initial work to jumpstart a teetering economy has brought tremendous results. The stock market surged to set new records. Unemployment has plummeted to the lowest mark in decades. The marketplace is moving again.

3. *Pro-life Policy*—Support for abortion is literally being erased from government policy across the spectrum. We have shifted from a covenant of death empowering a culture of death to a

covenant of life empowering a culture of life.

4. *Military Re-strengthened*—The decline of our military through an entire decade is being reversed. Honor, respect and care for our soldiers and veterans is a top priority demonstrated by this administration.

5. *Judicial Revolution*—The seating of Neil Gorsuch on the Supreme Court within Trump's first 100 days set an historic precedent. But there's more. Congress has paved the way for the Trump Administration to seat more federal judiciary appointees than any president in the previous 40 years. Truly a judicial revolution.

6. *United Nations Checked*—Led by UN ambassador Nikki Haley, major policy shifts have checked the thrust of anti-Semitism within the global body. Ambassador Haley has also worked to redirect funding to counter the abuses of dictatorships, as well as empowering the rights of women.

7. *Respect, Influence of Faith Community Restored*—Whereas previous administrations marginalized both the influence and values of the faith community, the Trump administration has openly promoted their ties. Further, advisors from the faith community have played a key role in shaping policy to help advance our nation. A genuine turnaround!

8. *Johnson Amendment repealed*—During the 2017 National Day of Prayer, President Trump announced his executive order repealing the Johnson Amendment, which put severe but as-yet-unenforced restrictions on the faith community in regards to influencing the political world. Restraints now off, the Constitutional mandate of separation of church and state has been restored to its original intent.

9. *Constitutional sovereignty upheld*—The Trump administration

has restored homeland security by honoring and enforcing both constitutional boundaries and the geographic boundaries of our nation.

10. *Restoring Christmas*—"We are stopping cold the attacks on Judeo-Christian values," Trump declared at the 2017 Value Voters Summit. "They don't use the word Christmas because it is not politically correct... We're saying Merry Christmas again!" I'm simply including this because of the clear reference to Christmas in the prophecy you'll read below. Can't make this stuff up.

Your Turnaround Verdict

I hope you can see the magnitude of the potential God is offering us through this Turnaround Verdict. Three dramatic elections all turned on a dime, with longstanding results. We have also seen dramatic turnarounds in our personal lives, our childrens' lives, and our ministry spheres. What I want to emphasize to you here is that if God is powerful enough to turn three major elections, He can absolutely bring a turnaround in your own life as well. But you have a key role in positioning your life and sphere to receive it!

Follow the pattern of the Maccabees. Separate from darkness—divorce Baal. Renew covenant with the Lord Jesus Christ as the foundation for your sphere. Approach the Bench with God's "turnaround verdict," applying it directly to your life.

And then get ready for a dramatic turnaround which launches your new beginning. Even in a midnight hour.

Trump Wins Contract: Dream January 5, 2016

Lets close out the "Midnight Turnaround" with a posting which conveys the prophetic potential being offered to the Trump presidency.

Donald Trump was just a candidate among many when, on January 5, 2016, the Lord gave me a dream which summed up the potential the Lord was offering our nation. We immediately knew Trump was selected to be a catalyst of the turnaround we were seeking. The most important part of the dream paints a picture of how all races of

Americans would be empowered, with new doors opening for success.

Finally, we saw through this dream how the Lord wanted to even restore our Judeo-Christian roots within our culture. Below is the posting from January 5, 2016 as it was originally written and published. God is amazing!

Turnaround Tuesday... Trump?

Throughout this prayer project we will be posting "real-time revelation" as the Lord grants it. This morning I had a very important dream. And I don't believe it's coincidence we are on our 45th Tuesday until the 45th presidential election, on our first Turnaround Tuesday.

The dream featured Donald Trump. Please note I am by no means advocating or endorsing any political candidate. Nor am I saying the Lord has made clear His choice for a political candidate. From my perspective, I believe each candidate in the running has the potential to be a great president, but each must overcome key challenges to embrace the greatness the Lord is offering them. For instance, Ben Carson must truly find his voice. Hilary Clinton must recover her genuine devotion. Marco Rubio must recover his compass. Ted Cruz must expand his vision.

And Donald Trump must become a statesman. My opinion only.

The Dream

That said, here's the dream. I was working at my former job as a contractor at the National Emergency Training Center. For five years, I served as a graphic designer and photographer there for the Department of Homeland Security/ FEMA.

And in the dream, it was Christmas-time, and Donald Trump had just won the contract for the center.

Trump came into the office with a few of his colleagues and looked around. The senior employees, including me, were acknowledged but not spoken to. I honestly felt insulted.

Insulted by Donald Trump. Imagine that. This dream does have some authenticity.

Donald Trump, the new contract manager, then took my son Jonathan and went to another wing of the building. Jonathan never worked at the training center, but in the dream he was a newcomer to the contract. The next generation.

I watched through a window as Trump and my son worked to renovate offices that were once occupied by great employees, but now were held by very lazy people. One of them was even tied to the occult.

When Trump came back through, he again spoke nothing. I reached out to him and said, "You must restore Christmas!" He just looked at me, almost amused, and nodded. My son, following behind, replied "Dad, that's just what we've been doing over there."

As we were talking, former colleagues began to come back through the doors. One was a bright, big-spirited African American woman. All the other employees greeted her with a sign by raising their elbows in the air. She raised hers in response, then stretched out her arms and locked her hands together as if in prayer. She was beaming as she was welcomed back to the job she was forced out of!

As she and other African American and Hispanic women began to come back through the doors, I realized in the dream that Donald Trump was actually cleaning out government offices and re-hiring excellent former employees that had been unfairly treated in previous seasons, primarily for their faith.

Then I woke up. Let me share a few brief points, then I'll leave the interpretation up to you.

Homeland Security Top Priority

The dream by no means openly conveyed that Donald Trump had become President. Specifically in the dream, Trump had won a contract for the Department of Homeland Security.

What is God saying? I believe a firm stand regarding the security of our homeland is essential to appeal to America's voters, whatever the party. The security of our homeland is top priority.

Is this good or bad? Both. I do believe it was prophetic that the location for the contract was the "National Emergency Training Center." Because we are in a season of training, where competencies and strategies are being refined to better answer the real-life challenges ahead.

Storms are brewing that threaten not only our nation but the entire western world. And previous training has uncovered a terrible potential. If we're not careful, the quest for the security of our homeland could become the primary force that pushes us into dictatorship.

As Benjamin Franklin noted, *"He who sacrifices freedom for security DESERVES NEITHER."* It's time to find the balance.

You're HIRED!

The dream also conveyed how many capable and industrious workers have been treated wrongfully, recently especially, for their embrace of Jesus Christ. The majority of believers I connected with during my time in government contracting were African American. They were very simply the strongest intercessors in their spheres.

I believe we're going to see a resurgence of devoted believers, competent above their peers like Daniel, returning to government offices. They're going to pass the tests that even the Donald Trumps of this world demand. Promotions that have been withheld will be released. YOU'RE HIRED!

You Must Restore Christmas

"You Must Restore Christmas!" There are many meanings within this simple statement. First in my heart is a statement from the Chronicles of Narnia by CS Lewis. When leaders become gateways for the enemy, the result is that it's *"always winter, and never Christmas."* In this respect especially, beloved it's time for Christmas to be restored!

I also believe God is compelling all Christians to actually give themselves to restoring Christmas as a celebration that again attracts the world to Jesus. From Washington to Washington to Jerusalem!

Pray Through the Coming Shift

The final point I want to make is that by Christmas next year, a new President will have been elected. A new President will be focused on building a new team for a new government.

And it's our job to pray NOW for this coming shift. First that it will fully occur. Secondly that the seats of authority from the President down will be filled with men and women of great capability and unyielding faith. Because that's exactly what it will take to access the opportunities and overcome the challenges we are faced with.

Re-constitution. Turnaround. No King but Jesus!

CHAPTER SIX
Turning the Tables

We began the last chapter by sharing a how the Lord is highlighting the Table of the Lord in this season. His table of covenant never loses its brilliance, even during your darkest hour. You can always depend on the body and blood of Jesus to attain for you a favorable verdict from God's Throne!

And you always have a seat at His table.

Further, you can depend on Him to turn the tables on your enemy. That's a benefit of your covenant with Him. Deliverance from the hand of every adversary! (II Kings 17:38-39).

Remember, Daniel 7:22 declares how His verdict of justice has been rendered in favor of the saints, restraining the beast and releasing His cherished people to possess the Kingdom. We call this the "Turnaround Verdict." Mostly because the Scripture conveys how a marginalized and subjugated people will be released into their covenant destiny as part of the execution of God's justice.

We've received just a taste of this in our own time. In conjunction with the prayers of the saints, God is turning the tables. In your own life first!

Turning the Tables, Exposing the Betrayer

"Betrayers will be exposed. They will fall in the fall of 2017!" Jolene received this word and assignment regarding the exposure of betrayal during a prophetic experience in August 2017, just before we launched our second Glory Train journey. The public focus of the Glory Train project was seeing the restoration of God's glory. But we also carried a private assignment—all across the continent.

The Lord showed Jolene we needed to receive communion at every stop along the way of our tour, declaring that God was covenantally releasing the exposure of systemic, intentional betrayal within the body of Christ and our world.

We carried this focus privately from coast to coast, and then continued the project publicly with the Lamplighter family through the Turning Tables Prayer Project. We felt to culminate the project on the last day of fall. Which happened to be December 20, our anniversary. In 2017 it also happened to mark the final day Hanukkah.

It is interesting that Hugh Hefner died the very day we completed our national journey, rolling into California. Jonathan Ngai, a longtime Hollywood minister, told us that three years beforehand the Lord clearly showed him that Hugh Hefner was the "strongman" of Hollywood, and that when he was removed a lot of hidden abuse would be exposed. It proved more true than we could possibly imagine.

Soon betrayal at the highest levels began to be exposed almost every day, from Hollywood to Washington DC and New York City.

The New Yorker and New York Times broke stories about sexual abuse by producers such as Harvey Weinstein against many of our nation's most prominent actresses. Many came out of the shadows afterwards. Exposing sexual harassment, rape, even pedophilia by Hollywood producers and actors such as John Lassater, Kevin Spacey and Ben Affleck. Soon after, exposure of extraordinary cover-ups by the Clintons, by Congressional leaders such as Sen. Al Frankena and Rep. John Conyers, news leaders such as Matt Lauer and Charlie Rose, all came to light.

Many more have followed. For months on end now.

We are grateful to the Lord Jesus for His redemptive exposure! Let me be clear that we are also deeply saddened by the extraordinary proliferation of such abuse at the highest levels of power. This process of exposure must continue. Lets ask God for His anointing of holy conviction to continue penetrating hearts across the land.

Before we go any farther, let me be clear that many in the body of Christ have been carrying similar assignments from the Lord, praying into these issues for years, even decades. We are celebrating every contribution as we move forward towards God's common goal.

Jolene's Prophetic Experience

Here is Jolene's prophetic experience on turning the tables, in her own words.

I (Jolene) was at my prayer group in Frederick MD where I had the following experience. It was early August, right before we started the second tour of the Glory train. It was a very intense day of prayer and many women showed up on this particular day that usually for one reason or another can't usually come. So we had noted that there were eleven of us that day which became very important later in this experience.

The prayer group was praying for North Korea at the time but I was silently asking the Lord to heal some pain in my feet that I had been experiencing. I was holding my feet up off the ground when I felt the actual presence of Jesus Himself entered the room. As in most experiences it is hard to convey what happens in the supernatural but I will do my best.

Jesus Washes Her Feet

In my experience He lifted my feet up and began to wash them, which was a very humbling experience. Exactly at that time I had the very same sense that Peter had that I should be washing His feet not the other way around. Then in the spirit the entire conversation with Peter, recorded as part of Christ's Last Supper, began to play out with the Lord. When I began to protest he said "What I am doing you do not understand now, but you will know after this." I have read this account many times but the exact wording of the John 13 scenario played out between me and Jesus. Please read the passage through. Here's how it begins:

"During supper, the devil having already put into the heart of Judas Iscariot, the son of Simon, to betray Him, Jesus, knowing that the Father had given all things into His hands, and that He had come forth from God and was going back to God, got up from supper, and laid aside His garments; and taking a towel, He girded Himself. Then He poured water into the basin, and began to wash the disciples' feet" (John 13:2-5).

The Last Supper—Communion

While reading John 13, there also seemed to be a supernatural illumination of the Word as I got to the part of Jesus sharing communion with his disciples. The Book of John I then felt led to take communion with the 11 women in the room just like Jesus did at His Last Supper (see Matthew 26:17-40, Mark 14:12-26, Luke 22:7-38). But I also became aware that the same communion that drew the 11 true disciples to Jesus was also what the Lord used to expose Judas as his betrayer.

I love how Luke records this moment: And he took bread, and when he had given thanks, he broke it and gave it to them, saying, "This is my body, which is given for you. Do this in remembrance of me." And likewise the cup after they had eaten, saying, "This cup that is poured out for you is the new covenant in my blood. But behold, the hand of him who betrays me is with me on the table. For the Son of Man goes as it has been determined, but woe to that man by whom he is betrayed!" (Luke 22:19-22).

Prophetic Action—Extending the Bread

So in a prophetic act I felt to call in all the true disciples of the Lord through communion. To gather, as it were, the eleven faithful disciples to Jesus.

I then felt to also extend the same bread and wine to those who are in the midst of betraying Jesus. I felt Jesus was using me to be His hands and His heart at that time. It was one of the most powerful communions

I have ever taken and I felt a very grave sense that much had shifted in the spirit realm and the betrayal of the enemy even through human agents would begin to be exposed in many situations and in the nation. Some will repent. But there are some betrayers who are sold out infiltrators, committed to the enemy's work.

And I knew the Lord was calling us to receive communion across the nation on the Glory Train. From city to city, this was to be a private witness before Heaven that those sold out to betrayal must now be exposed.

They Will Fall in the Fall

Jon and I went to Bethlehem, Pennsylvania a week later and the Lord reminded me of the experience as I felt the sadness of the enemy's infiltration in that beautiful Moravian town. I shared the story of my experience with Jesus in communion and asked for the enemy to be exposed there as well. Three days later I had a dream where Holy Spirit instructed me about infiltrators in the camp that needed to be exposed. In short He spoke to me that the betrayers, the infiltrators in the camp, WILL BEGIN TO FALL IN THE FALL.

I feel that the most important thing the Lord asked us to do on the Glory Train was to take communion across America with this focus. Drawing the 11 faithful to Jesus. And extending the bread to expose those who are intentionally betraying Christ's heart and cause at this time, both in His body and in our nation.

The purging actually begins with us. If we were truthful, each of us has unredeemed pockets of betrayal in our own hearts. Can your loyalty to Jesus be bought or sold? Lets ask God to create in us a clean heart, and renew a right spirit within us.

I also feel God wants us to engage together with Him—drawing close to Jesus in intimate communion, and also seeking Him to expose the betrayer. Some might want to set a goal and receive communion every day for the 21 days, just as we did with our Turning Tables Prayer Project. Lets draw close in intimacy with the Lord! And also lets plead for justice breakthroughs for His people and world.

The Lord showed Jon that the Table of the Lord is the highest court in the Kingdom of God. Please approach the bench, seeking the Lord for the willful betrayers to become exposed. Jesus desires to advance us beyond the sabotage the enemy has planned. IT'S TIME TO TURN THE TABLES!

Exposure: Sign That Awakening Has Begun!

Back in 2013, our book Crown & Throne chronicled a prophetic word the Lord had given us for 2015 and beyond. "The Third Great Awakening is a Great Return, where multitudes will disengage from Jezebel's table and return to the Table of the Lord." We wrote:

> "Just as God confronted Pharaoh in Egypt, so He is confronting the pushers, pimps, politicians, and power brokers behind Jezebel's table in our time. The journey from slavery to freedom in Exodus is the same journey from Jezebel's table to the table of the Lord that multitudes will be making today. He is rescuing Hosea's girl! She will disengage from the compromise, addictions, and covenant breaking she has embraced, and return to the secure refuge afforded by the table of the Lord" (Crown & Throne, pg. 196).

Jolene and I felt then that Jezebel's table of seduction would be exposed for what it is and overthrown. I believe that this redemptive exposure from Washington DC to Hollywood is part of this process. A genuine sign that the Third Great Awakening has indeed begun!

Table of Covenant

Sometimes in our haste, we forget that Jesus is a God of covenant. And the Table of the Lord is a table of covenant. It's like a banquet table at a wedding feast. You should only be seated next to the Bridegroom if you have pledged your loyalty to Him in marriage.

And it's in context with this marital covenant that God promises to deliver us from the hand of our adversaries. "The covenant I have made with you, you shall not forget, nor shall you fear other gods. But the Lord your God you shall fear, and He shall deliver you from the hand of all your enemies" (II Kings 17:38-9).

What does it mean to be married to Jesus? Two words come immediately to mind. Love and covenant. Through the covenant forged with His own body and blood, you and I are forgiven of our sins. Ransomed and redeemed. Joined with Jesus forever (see Isaiah 53).

"For the joy that was set before Him He endured the cross, despising the shame (Hebrews 12:2)." You are His passion, His joy! Please know He did not trade His life for yours merely out of obligation. Nor was His cross some kind of self-centered act of bravado driven by insecurity, a mission to prove His love and somehow win your affection.

No proof needed.

Jesus is love—in the purest form. As King He entered into an agony far beyond what any human being could ever comprehend, understanding the stakes temporally and eternally were greater than any human being could ever comprehend. Even at a time when those who were closest to Him in His life and ministry abandoned Him.

Don't think that He did not feel the weight of this betrayal. And don't think the shame you feel when you've been betrayed has somehow eluded His heart. He can fully empathize because He felt it Himself. He despised it. And yet He drank the cup to the fullest. This was part of the price He paid you and me, to secure us in Him forever.

Entire movements today are focused on intimacy with Jesus. But to a large extent we have become much like the world. Seeking the pleasure of intimacy divorced from the responsibilities of covenant. And that at the core is betrayal.

Lets return to wholehearted devotion. As the lover in the Song of Songs declared, "I am my beloved's and He is mine" (Song of Songs 6:3). We cannot have sustained, genuine intimacy without genuine covenant which is walked out in life.

Table of Justice

The Table of the Lord is also a table of His justice. I'll never forget a moment which changed my life forever. It changed how I viewed the Lord, and how I viewed communion. The Holy Spirit spoke to me a simple phrase. "The Table of the Lord is the highest court in the Kingdom of God."

As you become seated at the Table of the Lord on earth, so you become seated with Christ in heavenly places. And the Court which is above every court, including the Supreme Court, can be accessed by you immediately.

It is on this Table which, after His resurrection, Jesus presented His own body and blood for the redemption of mankind. The prophet Daniel chronicles this sacred moment:

> I kept watching in the night visions, and behold,
> with the clouds of heaven, One like a Son of Man
> was coming, and He came up to the Ancient of Days
> and was presented before Him (Daniel 7:13).

Daniel sees Jesus Christ, Israel's Messiah, appearing before the Court of Heaven immediately after His death and resurrection. Note that the Son of Man was presented before the Ancient of Days. To be presented to a person means that you are being relationally introduced. But to be presented before a person means you are being evaluated. There's an important difference.

In Daniel's vision, evidence was being presented before the Judge. Entered into the Court for consideration.

What was the evidence? Jesus spoke of it to His disciples on the night He was betrayed. He held up the Passover Cup and declared, "This is the blood of My covenant." He consecrated bread, and said, "This is my body, given for you." His own body and blood were being offered, for their redemption and ours. According to the prophet Isaiah:

> He was wounded for our transgressions, bruised for our
> iniquities, the chastisement that brought us peace was
> laid upon Him, and with His stripes we are healed...
> By His knowledge the Righteous One will justify many,
> for He will bear their iniquities (Isaiah 53:5, 11).

Through his prophetic vision, Isaiah conveys how our lawyer, our intercessor, would literally become the evidence for our legal justification. The prophet Daniel brings us right into the Courtroom scene where this same Son of Man presents His own body and blood for our redemption.

And when Messiah's blood and battered body was evaluated as evidence before Heaven's Court, judgement for all eternity was rendered in favor of the saints. Covenant was restored, and your turnaround was forever legally secured! Below is the verdict.

> And to Him was given dominion, Glory and a kingdom,
> that all the peoples, nations and men of every language
> might serve Him. And His dominion is an everlasting
> dominion, which will not pass away; and His kingdom
> is one which will not be destroyed" (Daniel 7:14).

If you remember one thing from this chapter, if only one sentence is allowed to become etched upon your heart and mind, let it be this. Jesus died and rose again to obtain for you a better verdict.

As we noted in our book Crown & Throne:

> "In the courtroom scene, a verdict was rendered—for Jesus
> and for you. First and foremost this was a marriage covenant,
> just as the first covenant with Israel had been. The Son of Man
> gained a bride, and you gained forgiveness, cleansing, healing
> and eternal life. The Son of Man gained a throne, and you
> became seated with your Bridegroom in heavenly places. The
> Son of Man gained a Kingdom, and you gained an inheritance,
> vast and eternal. The Son of Man gained dominion, and you
> gained a crown and throne" (Crown & Throne, pp. 90-91).

And because of this incredible gift of His body and blood, you and I can receive verdicts today which release Heaven's justice to our world. Truly—No King but Jesus.

Turning the Tables—Mary, Martha and Lazarus

Jesus went to such extraordinary depths to redeem you—and to redeem your destiny. Lets now see how the Lord turned the tables on behalf of a few of His closest friends on earth.

You probably know the story. But there's more to it than you might have perceived. Mary, Martha and Lazarus welcomed Jesus into their home. Mary sat at His feet, listening to His word. A crisis came when Lazarus died, compelling Jesus to perform perhaps His most extraordinary miracle. Mary and Martha held a banquet. And Mary poured out precious oil—spikenard—at the feet of Jesus.

It's vitally important for you to understand that the most transformative moments occurred while Mary was seated before Jesus. Quite literally, at the Table of the Lord. Lets pick up the story in Luke 10.

> "Now as they were traveling along, He entered a village; and a woman named Martha welcomed Him into her home. She had a sister called Mary, who was seated at the Lord's feet, listening to His word. But Martha was distracted with all her preparations; and she came up to Him and said, "Lord, do You not care that my sister has left me to do all the serving alone? Then tell her to help me."
>
> But the Lord answered and said to her, "Martha, Martha, you are worried and bothered about so many things; but only one thing is necessary, for Mary has chosen the good part, which shall not be taken away from her" (Luke 10:38-42).

Mary in this sequence is pictured as a "friend of the Bridegroom," seated at His feet and attentive to hear His voice. She took her seat at the table simply to behold Him. Martha in this story is pictured as restlessly striving to bless Jesus through her works.

Please keep this in mind. Mary is not. She is actually withholding from serving Jesus or giving anything to Him. She is in receiving mode only.

It's interesting how the Lord responds to them both.

"You are worried and bothered about so many things,
Martha. But Mary has chosen to commune with me. She
made a great decision. She chose the one thing necessary.
That is to sit before Me and listen to My word. And the
growth of our relationship must remain uninterrupted."

Many lovers of God are entering into such a season right now. It's time to set aside distractions which make you worried and burdened. Take a break from the news. Take your seat at the Table of the Lord. Commune with the whispers of your King.

Be like Mary and choose the one thing. Behold the Bridegroom.

Family Background

Here's some important background information. Mary had accumulated a substantive amount of spikenard, worth about a year's wages. It was probably her valuable possession. In his book "Passion for Jesus," Mike Bickle suggests that it might have come as an inheritance from her parents (Passion for Jesus, pg. 200). I agree.

Mike points out that when Jesus came to Bethany, He identified the home as Martha's possession. It was highly unusual at that time for a woman to own real estate. Most likely the parents of Mary, Martha and Lazarus had died prematurely. Lazarus was probably too young to qualify for the inheritance. The home most likely went to Martha, and an inheritance of spikenard to Mary.

Mary and Martha were probably both tasked with raising Lazarus into manhood. That said, all three were suffering from the loss of their parents. Most likely all three felt extremely abandoned, even by God.

And it was to these three that Jesus was drawn.

Mary's Moment with Jesus

Mary chose the one thing necessary—to sit at His feet. I often wonder about the substance of their conversation. This is merely speculation, but based on personal revelation I can give an educated guess. Because in the Song of Songs, another bride is also pictured as seated at the feet of her beloved. And just like Mary, she possessed a costly treasure of perfumed oil.

"While the king was at His table, my spikenard gave forth its fragrance. My beloved to me is a pouch of myrrh, which lies all night between my breasts. My beloved is to me a cluster of henna blossoms in the fields" (SoS 112-14).

That said, I can almost hear the conversation between Jesus and Mary, with His friend seated at His table.

"I love you, Lord… Please take me deeper in our relationship"

"I love you too, Mary. More than you can possibly understand."

"Lazarus is grown now. My responsibilities have mostly been fulfilled. Maybe we can spend more time together. I know you have your disciples and everything. But Jesus, with all your ministry travels you really need a companion."

"You might still be needed here."

"But I need to be with you."

"Me too, Mary. I really do. Just not as you understand right now."

"I've heard that before from men."

"Mary… your love is genuine, and I delight in it. I love spending time with you. You know me better than most anyone in the world. I have chosen you. And I'm about to expand your heart even more. Let me show you how your own story has been woven into God's word."

My guess is that Mary received revelation from Jesus about the trial which would test both their hearts in coming days. And in the midst of His unfolding story, she learned that day about the eternal significance of her own inheritance. While the king was seated at his table…

Spikenard. The oil of the bride.

Myrrh. The oil of suffering. Of a midnight crisis. The oil of remembrance.

Henna. A cluster of flowers which symbolizes resurrection.

The Midnight Crisis

Not too long after they visited, Mary and Martha suffered another family crisis. Lazarus became sick. This chronicle is recorded in John 11. The sisters issued a midnight cry for Lazarus—a desperate call for Jesus to come and attend to him. "Lord, he whom you love is sick."

Jesus responded with a prophetic word. "This sickness is not to end in death, but for the Glory of God, so that the Son of God may be glorified by it."

Glory. One of the most puzzling scriptures in the entire canon of the Bible is that "Jesus loved Martha and her sister and Lazarus. So when He heard that he was sick, He stayed two days longer in the place where He was."

Jesus delayed. And Lazarus drew his last breath.

Of course, that's when the Lord decided to go see his friend. Watch this now. In this case, Jesus' word alone did not bring Lazarus' healing. Jesus had to go on a journey for His own word to be manifested. Sometimes we will have to make a journey as well. We might have to pray onsite.

Turning the Tables

Please note that to even make this journey, Jesus was putting his own life at risk. The disciples mentioned this to Him. "Rabbi, the Jews were just seeking to stone you. And you want to go again?"

Jesus' reply stunned them. "Lazarus our friend has fallen asleep. I go that I may awaken him from slumber" (John 11:11).

Lazarus was dead. But Jesus was sent to awaken him from slumber! In this passage Jesus forever defines the awakening He longs to bring to mankind. It's more than just goosebumps at a revival. Jesus wants to shift us from death to life! It's not a coincidence that we are contending for this shift right now. From a covenant of death empowering a culture of death to a covenant of life empowering a culture of life.

You might even note that the Pilgrims cut covenant with the Lord on 11-11, 1620 for the land and government of this nation. We are a nation of awakening! And on the 400th anniversary of their covenant we are going to see His glory. Lazarus come forth!

Jesus at the Gate

Remember this is the year of the gate. Your decisions to go to the gate, and your decisions at the gate, will set the course for your future. Both Martha and Mary were required to go to the gate of Bethany to meet Jesus. And it was at this gate where the power of delay, the power of deferred hopes, was overcome and broken off. Watch how Jesus comes to your most contested gate this year and compels you to usher Him through!

When Jesus finally arrived in Bethany, Martha ran to meet Him at the gate. But Mary—the lover of God, the friend of the Bridegroom—remained in the house of mourning. Like the virgins who fell asleep when the Bridegroom delayed, Mary had succumbed to her grief.

> WATCH HOW JESUS COMES TO YOUR MOST CONTESTED GATE THIS YEAR AND COMPELS YOU TO USHER HIM THROUGH!

Who could blame her. She had lost her parents, and now she had lost Lazarus. The Man she probably hoped would one day be her husband had abandoned her. Not even bothering to come and tell His friend goodbye, let alone heal him when all knew He was fully capable of doing so. Intimacy was betrayed. Trust violated. At least that was her assumption.

Despite her despair, Martha ran to meet Jesus. And she actually was renewed in revelation. Their conversation is fascinating.

"Lord, if you had been here my brother would not have died. Even now I know that whatever You ask of God, God will give You."

"Your brother will rise again."

"I know that the will rise again in the resurrection at the last day."

"Martha… I AM the resurrection and the life. He who believes in Me will live even if he dies. And everyone who lives and believes in Me will never die. Do you believe this?"

Martha's reply was stunning. "Yes Lord; I have believed that You are the Christ, the Son of God, even He who comes into the world."

What? Where did Martha gain this revelation? This woman so busy and worried had somehow gained a buoyancy in her spirit which carried her through even her time of grief. Her lamp was burning with fresh revelation. There's a reason she ran to meet Jesus at the gate! She saw Jesus in a new way—as Israel's promised Messiah.

"Mary has chosen the one thing necessary. And it will not be taken from her." Remember those words were addressed to Martha. Declaring that she too was welcome to sit at His feet and listen to His word. Martha took the advice. She too began to still herself and sit at the Table of the Lord.

And He filled her with revelation.

Martha was also very wise. Note how she returned to Mary and gently summoned her. Martha's message is exactly the same as that of the midnight rider, compelling Mary to rise up and meet Him. "The Teacher is here, Mary. And He's calling for you."

It's very interesting that Jesus had not yet moved into the village. He was still right where Martha left Him, still at the gate. There is something so important about meeting Jesus at the gate this year that He will even refrain from moving until all of His closest friends have a chance to meet Him and welcome Him in.

Mary fell at His feet, weeping. "Lord, if You had been here, my brother would not have died." Her anguish moved Jesus deeply. He knew the love she carried in her heart for Him, and that she was wrestling through the sense that by not coming, He had betrayed her trust. Her heart. Her love.

Jesus wept.

And Lazarus awakened. He came forth from the dead.

What most people miss about the story is that by resurrecting Lazarus, Jesus signed His own death warrant. It was one thing to heal a fever or drive out a demon. It was another thing entirely for a man known by everyone to be brought back to life. Nobody could accomplish this but Messiah. This was revolutionary—in a way which threatened the longstanding seats of religious authority, and even the seat of government itself. Jesus was now a threat to Roman rule. This "Messiah of Israel" must be stopped.

In a very real way, Lazarus' resurrection cost Jesus His life.

Love Poured Out

Jesus soon took his final journey. Six days before the Passover, He came to Bethany and visited with Martha, Mary and Lazarus. Scripture says that they made Him supper that day. Martha and Mary both served Him (John 12:2).

This is important. Though Mary loved Jesus, she was never pictured serving Him. Until now.

What changed? Her heart. When Lazarus arose, her own heart awakened too. Her vision was made new. Mary no longer saw Jesus as betraying her or disenfranchising her through circumstances of life. The pain of past loss and deferred hopes was healed. Instead, she gained in her spirit a resolute trust in Jesus which even transcended the grave.

And she was free to express her love by serving Him.

I believe Mary served even knowing what would soon take place in Jesus' life. My Spirit-empowered guess is that she saw in Lazarus what would soon happen to her Beloved. She knew the resurrection of her brother stirred the government to take Him down. And she knew also that Jesus had come to visit just before Passover.

Perhaps she recalled the conversation they had together shortly before her world turned upside down.

"I need to be with you."

"Me too, Mary. I really do. Just not as you understand right now... Let me show you how your own story has been woven into God's word."

Myrrh. My beloved is a bundle of myrrh, which lies all night between my breasts. My beloved is going to die soon. He and I both will go through a very dark night, as Jesus exchanges His life for me.

Henna. Resurrection. A love stronger than death. He will live again, and I will be with Him eternally.

Spikenard. The fragrant oil of a cherished bride. While the king sat at his table...

This beloved woman soon gave Jesus her most treasured possession. "Mary took a pound of very costly perfume of pure spikenard, and anointed the feet of Jesus and wiped His feet with her hair; and the house was filled with the fragrance of the perfume" (John 12:4).

Mary poured out on Jesus all she had lived to gain and protect—to a Man who was about to die. The fragrance of the bride. The oil of her worship soon filled the entire house.

Judas scolded Jesus for receiving the outpouring of Mary's love. The oil valued at a year's wages should have gone to the poor, he said. "Now he said this, not because he was concerned about the poor, but because he was a thief, and as he had the money box, he used to pilfer what was put into it" (John 12:6).

Note that Judas' betrayal did not begin at the Last Supper. It actually began with literally robbing God. Really an important point to ponder.

But Jesus' response is telling. He said she anointed Him for the day of His burial.

Six days later, Jesus found Himself in a solitary garden on the side of the Mount of Olives facing the Temple Mount, His own sweat mixed with blood due to His anguished cry. He was about to turn the tables on behalf of all mankind. But at the moment it seemed the exact anthesis was occurring.

The Covenant Keeper was betrayed by His friend.

The King of Israel was captured by Roman soldiers.

The Lawgiver became subject to open defiance of God's heart and law.

The Eternal Judge received a death sentence.

And the Bridegroom gave His life for His bride.

Jesus became our Passover lamb. I submit to you that something powerful sustained Him to persevere on that cross. He saw you. He saw me. And He most likely rehearsed the memory of abandoned love by a bride who genuinely knew His heart. She gave her all to Him. And He was going to give His all to her.

"Forgive them, Lord, they know not what they do."

The Bible says Jesus was delivered over to death for our sins, and He was raised to life for our justification (Romans 4:25). Note that justification is a legal term. Remember, after Jesus' resurrection He presented His own body and blood on the mercy seat before His Throne.

Evidence before Heaven's Court that the highest price had now been paid, and that humanity could be forgiven. So that, as Misty Edwards sings, "the Father can have a family, and the Son can have a bride."

So that you and I could be completely redeemed. That's the ultimate turnaround.

Like Mary, you probably have some areas of your life that are still off limits even to God. Places where the pain or violation or trauma is so deep that you prefer nobody touch it, not even Him. It's tainted your perception of God, and it's tainted your perception of yourself.

If that's you, let me encourage you. There's an oil which can make your lamp burn again. There's a grace that soothes and heals. God's love brings both. He is not afraid of your raw honesty; in fact He prefers it.

And through Jesus alone, what the enemy meant for evil in your life can be turned for your ultimate good. He gave Himself completely to redeem you completely.

Take some time to sit at His table and receive. Pour out your heart. Pour out your love. Ask Him to cleanse and heal you of deferred hopes and dreams. And then ask Him to impart to you the resurrection power which has secured your presence with Him forever.

By His cross and resurrection, Jesus not only redeemed your life, but He also redeemed your destiny as well. You have gained a seat at His table. Covenant. Intimacy. Justice.

And royalty.

CHAPTER SEVEN
The Kingship Anointing

God is coming to the places where you have staked your covenant commitment to Him. And He is crowning your covenant commitment with His glory and His government!"

This word from the Lord, prophesying the release of His Kingship anointing came as thunder to me. So much so that my insides were quivering.

And it came at a most unexpected time. In August 2016 Jolene and I attended a solemn reunion of Christian leaders who had taken a special class on the Holocaust at Yad Vashem. We were discussing the resurgence of anti-Semitism in our day, including the use of the news media to spread false reports and fabricated propaganda to influence the masses in deception.

My fear was that, if the wrong candidate were to win the presidency, the lies and deceptive propaganda already empowering this resurgence would only be perpetuated. And probably strengthened.

Not on our watch. We were right in the middle of the 50 state

"Turnaround Tour," and took a break just to have our resolve re-empowered. Because the parallels between the globalist movement of Nazi Germany and the deceptive propaganda being welcomed by the masses in our hour was haunting.

All that noted, from a protocol perspective, a lecture on the Holocaust or Shoah was no place to shake and quiver under the power of God's visitation. My outside face remained stoic. My insides were bursting.

And God was making a point. At that very moment He was crowning the covenant commitment of those gathered. Nationally, at a crisis moment where we could either choose freedom or succumb to a globalist thrust again imperiling His covenant people, the Lord committed Himself to a turnaround. To the release of covenantal authority and anointing which governmentally catalyzes the turnaround and sees it through to completion.

To the Kingship anointing.

Because of this word, our Turnaround Tour suddenly made an unexpected turn. We actually journeyed to Israel and staked our covenant commitment into Zion's hill. Remember Your covenant, Lord. Remember Your Turnaround Verdict. Judgement in favor of the saints!

Our midnight cry from Zion, and from all 50 states, was soon met with results which seemed virtually impossible. Just as Netanyahu's election turned, so did the 2016 presidential elections. This was largely due to the influence of the Christian community, who voted in record numbers.

And we saw with our own eyes how God crowned the covenant commitment of so many intercessors with His glory and His government. Beloved, there's a crowning of His covenant people in this hour. Your royalty is being redeemed!

Daniel 7:22—Part Two

Remember Daniel 7:22, which we like to call the Turnaround Verdict. Judgement is rendered in favor of the saints, releasing the saints to possess the kingdom. Two facets of God's redemptive justice are conveyed here. The first is a turnaround for the saints. The second is actually the release of these same saints to possess the kingdom.

Note the progression. We have received a turnaround. Now you and I are being released to possess the Kingdom. In other words, to function with a Kingship anointing in our world.

For your review, Daniel 7:21 conveys how an antichrist horn was "waging war against the saints and overpowering them" (Daniel 7:21). Every step of faith was met with overwhelming resistance. Their worship was hindered. Their values were mocked in the public square. The saints became marginalized.

Finally the Ancient of Days takes His seat, and a verdict of justice is released in favor of the saints. Then these same disenfranchised, discouraged, broken people are suddenly released to possess the kingdom.

Beloved, that's the season we are in—right now. It's probably not a coincidence that well-known prophets such as James Goll have received words just this year about functioning as kings and kingmakers. And a hidden prophet whom Jolene and I greatly respect, Martin Frankena, felt a release from the Lord just this year to begin unpacking revelation he's been receiving over the past decade on Kingship.

And as we progress in stewarding this facet of God's new movement, it has the potential to impact our world even at a similar magnitude to the Protestant Reformation.

The Kingship Anointing

"And in these next ten years, as I have restored the harp and the bowl, I am going to further restore now the walking with the throne and the crown. I'm going to restore to My people walking in governmental intercessory, kingly authority. That what you proclaim on earth shall be that which you have already heard proclaimed in heaven!"

This prophetic word by Rick Ridings, declared over Washington DC in January 2012, became the revelatory inspiration for our book "Crown & Throne." And it sums up the extraordinary shift we have entered into in this season. Whereas the priestly ministry has been largely emphasized in previous seasons, the Lord is now beginning to unseal the scrolls of revelation regarding the kingly anointing. Intimacy, authority and influence. Governmental prayer which, as we have seen, can even change the course of nations.

A new order is emerging—kings and priests to our God, patterned like Jesus after the order of Melchizedek, who served as king and priest of Salem. We together will rule with Him in a way that brings Heaven's desires to the earth.

In his prophecy about the Crown & Throne movement, Rick Ridings explained how kingly, governmental intercession was actually an expansion of the Harp and Bowl movement centered on 24-7 worship and prayer before God's throne. This is pictured in Revelation 5:8—10.

> "When He had taken the book, the four living creatures
> and the twenty-four elders fell down before the Lamb,
> each one holding a harp and golden bowls full of
> incense, which are the prayers of the saints.
>
> And they sang a new song, saying, "You are worthy to take
> the scroll, and to open its seals; for You were slain, and have
> redeemed us to God by Your blood out of every tribe and tongue
> and people and nation, and have made us kings and priests to
> our God; and we shall reign on the earth" (Revelation 5:8-10).

Jesus made you both a king and a priest to your God. And a tremendous price was paid to obtain this facet of your redemption.

Outside the gates of Israel's ancient governmental capital, Jesus hung on a cross under a sign mocking him as King of the Jews. Blood streamed down His face from a mock crown, interspersed with thorns which was jammed into His skull. No scepter was in His hand. Instead the hands of this King of the Jews were nailed to a tree.

He was born as King. He was crucified as King. He was raised to life as King. And for this reason, the moment you received the body and blood of His covenant love, your name was entered into the scrolls of royalty before His Throne.

But beloved, it's one thing to discover you are royalty. It's another thing to function in the office. Especially if you've gone through a season like the saints went through as portrayed in Daniel 7. Disenfranchised, marginalized, forsaken… this doesn't seem to be training for reigning.

Or does it?

School of Kings

"Wax on, wax off. Wax on, wax off. Wax on, wax off!"

You remember "The Karate Kid." The classic movie opens with a young firebrand named Daniel getting massively bullied. Daniel is soon taken under wing by a wise old master of martial arts, cleverly disguised as an apartment handyman. Mr. Miyagi agrees to teach the kid how to defend himself.

I so wanted a mentor like that growing up. How about you?

And like Daniel, I bet you would have been outraged when the kid's mentor Miyagi immediately demanded extreme servitude from his new student. Want a lesson in karate? First go wax my antique car. No wait, my entire collection of antique cars.

Wax on, wax off. Wax on, wax off. Wax on, wax off!

Of course, when the impatient, mouthy, exhausted kid finally confronts the ancient master, the wisdom of his endless service suddenly becomes clear. Muscle memory rules. Because without even realizing it, the protege was intuitively learning core defensive moves which would soon make him a champion.

A king.

Jolene and I have been facilitating Schools of Kings across our nation, with the intention of helping God's people grow into their kingly identity and calling. And we've made a significant discovery. Long before we ever entered the picture, the Lord has already been mentoring you in the Kingship anointing. Not only does He have the ultimate warrior moves, but He's also a master trainer. Through highs and lows, and even in the midst of the mundane and menial tasks, He doesn't miss a moment to coach you in your calling.

Even when you don't know He's there.

David grew into his kingship by learning to be a shepherd. A Jewish rabbi named Saul got knocked off of his horse as the Lord confronted a root of hatred behind his extreme religious devotion. By God's grace and amazing earned authority, Paul went on to become the pre-eminent apostolic leader of his time. Most of the New Testament is attributed to his writings.

Moses may have learned leadership in Egypt, but it took 40 years in the wilderness for him to gain the humility to actually lead. Remember that God was delivering His people from the power of the pyramid— not into it. A point more than a few leaders should consider today.

And then there's Esther. A street kid taken in by Mordecai, a wise old master of life. Advanced by his tutelage, she soon competes in a beauty contest—and becomes the queen of Babylon.

As part of her preparation I'm sure Esther burned the midnight oil learning how to carry out the role of a queen. Diplomatic protocol. Leadership. Literature and culture. Hosting and entertaining. But the primary emphasis of her preparation was actually in the form of beauty treatments featuring oil baths. Six months of myrrh, six months of frankincense.

Myrrh, the fragrance of suffering. Frankincense, the fragrance of healing. Like Mary of Bethany, her training through the journey was ultimately for reigning.

As we approach the subject of the kingship anointing, the good news is that you've already been in training for reigning with Him without even knowing it. The challenging news is that there are no shortcuts to the progression that Jesus demands from each of us. The course He sets for you is always personally tailored. And it always mandates a forging of deeper humility within your heart.

Through it all your Master remains your greatest servant. And His mandate remains the same. Want to rule with Him? No King but Jesus! And no cross, no crown.

Wax on, wax off. Be faithful. Trust me, soon will it all make sense. Because as only He can, Jesus is going to crown your covenant commitment with His glory and His government.

Thrones of Governance—Eight Key Principles

"We're in a time of the coming glory! We're in a time of rain!" Prophet Bob Jones prophesied about the Kingship anointing in his classic message on the Glory Train. "I also believe it is the reign of a King. I believe that we're going to begin to anoint Jesus as King..."

This word really meant a lot to our Lamplighter community. For almost six years, we've been hosting weekly conference calls to pray over our nation. Each call begins and ends with a corporate declaration, "No King but Jesus!"

Because it's just that time.

Jesus' Kingship is reflected in our kingship. In other words, His rulership in and through our lives. As we've emphasized throughout the pages of the Midnight Cry, God wants you to establish your throne—or sphere of authority—by uncompromised covenant with Him.

As we've pursued releasing God's kingdom into governmental spheres in Washington DC, we've focused on eight key aspects of the Kingship anointing. Most are covered with much more depth in our book "Crown & Throne." Here is a quick overview to help you lay some tracks.

1. *Thrones are established by covenant*—In other words, covenants establish thrones of governance. The US Constitution is a great example of this. As a legally binding covenant for our nation, it establishes our thrones of governance and defines the functions, responsibilities, and boundaries of each governmental seat. On a more personal level, your seat or throne is also established by covenant! It was secured the moment you received Christ's covenant with you.

2. *Compromising our covenants also compromises our seats of authority*—This is again why we've been mandated by God to carry such an emphasis on covenant renewal through repentance. Including approaching the bench to divorce Baal. We actually sought the divorcement from Baal over each governmental seat of the White House, the House of Representatives, the Senate,

the Supreme Court, the State Department, the Pentagon, our intelligence communities, etc. Wherever covenant had been compromised, the enemy gained a foothold to rule. The gates of sabotage needed to be shut.

3. *God wants to shut the gates of sabotage in your own life—* It is vital to pursue healing and deliverance from present and generational bondages. This gift was purchased by Christ as part of the redemption of your destiny. He wants to give this to you now!

4. *God sets His people in thrones of governance to usher His kingdom into their sphere—*Sometimes this is through our natural government, or what we call the seven spheres of society. But sometimes not. Elijah was granted a throne of governmental authority over Israel which no natural ruler could either offer or take away from him. As God spoke to Jeremiah, so He is speaking to many of you today: *"Behold, I have put My words in your mouth. See, I have appointed you this day over the nations and over the kingdoms, to pluck up and to break down, to destroy and to overthrow, to build and to plant"* (Jeremiah 1:9-10).

5. *Jesus wants to relate to you out of your throne of authority—* Consider yourself part of the King's cabinet. Your seat at His table grants you unhindered access to an authority even greater than kings and presidents of earth. And just as the Lord relates to you in intimacy, so He wants to relate to you out of your sphere of responsibility.

6. *Are you available to Him? Even if it's inconvenient?* Imagine if America were under attack and the Secretary of Defense wasn't available to take the President's call. Disaster! In like fashion, we must make ourselves available to Him. In prayer and life, manmade agendas will do little to advance the Kingdom. Also

determine now to set your course according to Christ's direction alone. Not every opportunity is of the Lord. And if you leave just because things are difficult, you may abort the eternal purpose for which you are there. Be led by His Spirit!

7. *Are you responsible? In other words, are you faithful?* A person of integrity? The difference between spectator Christianity and making a difference in your world comes down to one simple word. Responsibility. Be willing to take responsibility in the kingdom, and see things through to completion. Only then will you redefine your world.

8. *Apostolic diplomacy is a mandate*—Most of the Biblical prophets prophesied into government, and into the lives of governmental leaders. I cannot emphasize enough the importance of genuine honor and discretion when interfacing at this level. So often people disqualify themselves because of presumption. Choose dialogue over preaching. Provide solutions that serve their best intentions. Be genuine.

Here's a final thought as you pursue the Kingship call and anointing. One encounter with Jesus is not enough! The strength of your kingship is first sustained by continually encountering your King. Remember the Lord threatened to remove the lampstands of His people if they did not return to first love devotion. He warns us all is for our own longterm success. Don't let your lamp become burned out.

Daniel & Esther—Prototypes for Today

Daniel the prophet and Esther the queen both provide incredible examples of the Kingship calling today. Both served with excellence in government—and they both served kings. Both lived in exile in Babylon, now the region of Iraq and Persia. And it's there that God encountered them both with revelation which brought dramatic turnarounds to their world. In Daniel's case, even the end of days was framed out by God's word.

And they both possessed an excellent spirit.

Recently the Holy Spirit showed Jolene how "Many in the body of Christ have been discipling others out of a wounded soul instead of an excellent spirit." In her own words, here are a few insights.

The statement hit me like a ton of bricks because of the truth of it. We all do the best that we can do in and of ourselves, but so often the power of Christ in us to produce glory in others is lessened by our wounds, dysfunction and lack of godly discipline. Sometimes we end up defiling the very treasures God wants to refine!

Both Daniel and Esther were known for having "an excellent spirit" (Daniel 6:3). God wanted us to again embrace discipline and refining in our lives, pursuing excellence in who we are and all we do. It is a very serious time we are entering into and we as the body of Christ are being put into a season of "Daniel training" so that the excellence in our spirit can rise above the wounds of our souls.

I want to share with you some of the insights the Lord has impressed upon me from my studies in Daniel. One of the first things the Lord spoke to me is that kings, or rulers, are going to begin to have warning dreams. It is a year where many in key positions in our country and others are facing challenges even to their leadership. The Lord is warning many ahead of time through dreams.

For a long time, prophets in the land have been receiving warning dreams. But now the dreams are also going to be released to those actually in authority. And in this season we are going to need a company of Daniels who will be able even to interpret dreams for the kings. The interpretations themselves will announce the Highest King's decrees.

Daniel 7:22 and the Ultimate Midnight Turnaround

Lets conclude our overview of the Kingship anointing with a final look at Daniel 7:22, otherwise known as the Turnaround Verdict. Throughout the world, we've been asked one consistent question as we've ministered on this message. Daniel's verdict—does it apply to his generation, or to the saints in the end of days as they face the antichrist, or to us?

The answer is—yes. Like the parable of the midnight cry itself, this passage finds its ultimate fulfillment in the end of days. But it clearly has incredible relevance right now, especially as Holy Spirit has been highlighting it.

Biblical records actually validate that the Turnaround Verdict was first applied to the very next generation after Daniel. Since he was a child, Daniel spent his entire life praying for God's people to be restored from exile in Babylon. He never saw it. But the generation after him did.

And a primary catalyst was a midnight turnaround in a midnight hour in which God's covenant people were about to face a holocaust.

Esther was queen at the time. She learned from her father and mentor Mordecai that a beast named Haman had gained legal permission to commit genocide against the Jewish people. As Esther pleaded her cause in her king's court, her case was also being heard before Heaven's Court. Judgement was rendered in favor of the saints, exposing the betrayer. Haman was hanged on his own noose.

And the saints were literally released to possess the kingdom. Esther was invited to rule over half of Babylon. And her people were soon released to possess their kingdom, the Promised Land. In the midst of the midnight crisis, a midnight cry brought a midnight turnaround from the Lord. A new decree of freedom was issued. And a covenant people made a glorious procession back to their homeland.

> AS ESTHER PLEADED HER CAUSE IN HER KING'S COURT, HER CASE WAS ALSO BEING HEARD BEFORE HEAVEN'S COURT. JUDGEMENT WAS RENDERED IN FAVOR OF THE SAINTS, EXPOSING THE BETRAYER

All that to say... anytime Holy Spirit emphasizes this Turnaround Verdict it is valid in Heaven's Court. And it will be enforced in the earth. But it will find ultimate fulfillment with a future generation of saints marked to shine through the final midnight crisis of the end times. When an antichrist spirit openly defies constitutional governance, betrays covenant, changes times and law, rules through deceit and retribution, persecutes the saints and unleashes immorality and evil on a level never before experienced.

Perhaps this is coming soon, perhaps not. We simply don't know. But if you just consider the signs of the times, you must concede that we've been moving closer towards this era.

To those who may actually find themselves living through the end-times, Jolene and I hope this book provides inspiration for you. We have been praying for you. Knowing that what the Lord has done in some small part through the release of this verdict in our time, He is going to release in full during your time in history. Though the enemy has tried to mark you for subjugation, the Lord has marked you for victory. It is our genuine hope you will find clarity, guidance and resolve that will equip you to advance through this midnight hour.

Be sure to approach the Bench and present your case. Remembering that the same God who judges in your favor will also make war to uphold His verdict on your behalf.

Even as you face down the most impossible odds.

Behold the Bridegroom. He's coming for you. Rise up to meet Him.

CHAPTER EIGHT
The Midnight Riders

Jolene and I now live across the street from the Pentagon. Probably not a coincidence that we pray a lot for our military and intelligence communities. And at the Pentagon, on an underground floor somewhere in America's largest office building, a 24-7 watch continues unabated over the entire globe. Data and reports pour in for analysts to prioritize. Eyes in the sky provide visuals of military campaigns, terror strikes, emerging threats and special ops missions.

All in real-time.

Back in 1775, America's capacities to convey intelligence may not have been quite so advanced. But they were all the more innovative. Paul Revere relied on real-time signals from the upper room of a church to convey troop movements during a British invasion of Boston. He then mounted his horse for a midnight ride to broadcast the intelligence he had received.

The American military awakened that night to a midnight cry. And the world would never be the same.

Especially over this season from 2018-2020, a midnight watch must continue unabated in the upper rooms of our churches and houses of prayer. Accurate signals must be received, analyzed and broadcast. Much attention must indeed be focused on emerging threats, terror strikes and even military movements as a very real conflict of thrones continues.

But we are also watching for advances that no government can restrain, nor can any natural army overcome. We are watching for the movement of the Lord. One that will even bring an awakening even to our military once again! Yes, I am prophesying here. No King but Jesus is the battle cry America's revolutionaries taught us to hold to. In the next few years the cry itself comes full circle!

And in the same way that Paul Revere was summoned to start the Revolution, so midnight riders are again being summoned with fresh, real-time intelligence to announce God's coming movements in the earth. Including the long-promised awakening, fueled by the restoration of God's glory in 2018-2020.

I have to emphasize—as we keep watch.

Lets look at two dreams with "real-time" intelligence on this. Signals to the forerunners that it is now time to ride.

Heaven is Ready to Ride! Trump Dream

In May 2016 the Lord gave me a second dream featuring Donald Trump. I saw President Trump on the home plate of a baseball diamond, hitting balls to fielders as part of batting practice and then connecting with key intercessors on the sidelines. Fierce storm clouds gathered and it got really dark. He walked off the field by himself towards the locker room, his team following at a distance.

I'll let the posting, from May 21, 2016, take it from here:

In the final part of the dream we were leaving the field after batting practice. I heard and felt the ground shake. Looking up I saw two white horses, strong steeds galloping right towards us on the field! One especially was looking right at me, with a look in his eyes I can only describe as a resolve of fierce delight.

My instinct was to get out of the way, but they were coming so quickly. And before I even could move, this one horse raced right to me and thrust his head into my hands and chest. I intuitively embraced him.

At that time, Donald Trump was walking by, wearing a blue blazer, tan pants and a red hat like the one he always wears which says, "Make America Great Again." He seemed completely absorbed in thought. With the team, but walking alone.

Trump came over, nodded, smiled and said very simply, "You gotta keep praying for me." Then I woke up.

I knew the dream overall conveyed a final thrust of victory. Heaven's horses were joining in to bring breakthrough! Which is why I titled the posting accordingly. And it came to pass.

But I also knew intuitively that the appearance of the horses represented a demarcation of a new season associated with the forerunner movement and an acceleration into end time events. The horses of the Lord were being released, even to us.

Here's something I didn't perceive. The dream concluded with a clear admonition to continue praying for then-candidate Trump. Just a year later, a Republican baseball practice came under fire from a gunman who had ultimately sought the new president's life. We should all heed the admonition carefully and pray for our president.

That said, Heaven's horses have now been sent to turn the tide and help us regain momentum, even through storms. Stay strong and stable on your governmental watch with the Lord. These horses are ushering us into a new season of great synergy with Heaven and advancement in your world.

Heaven is Ready to Ride! Jamie Jackson Dream

My friend Jamie Jackson also caught a glimpse of Heaven's preparation of midnight riders—oddly enough at a funeral. Jamie is a pastor of a powerful church in the small seaside town of Brunswick, Georgia. He had just finished speaking when all of the sudden the veil was rolled away, and he saw how Heaven's midnight riders were being prepared.

Jamie writes: *"I spent a few moments talking about the road that Jack had traveled over the past few years and that he had traveled it well. As I concluded, I wanted to convey a little of what he's experiencing now. "With all the technology that we currently have, watching our big flat screen in high definition showing the most brilliant detailed colors yet… NONE OF THIS CAN COMPARE to what Jack is seeing today!"*

I closed my part in prayer and made my way back to my seat. Then suddenly things began to change. Once I set down the Lord took me into a vision, one like I've never seen.

The room I'm in changes and I'm now standing at the gates of Heaven. Most would ask about the details of the gates but I don't remember much except I remember how big they where. As I stood before them I was thinking the gates are the size of buildings and that there is nothing that was ever created by man that couldn't fit through these massive gates.

The Lord brought my attention to the opening of the gates where I saw Jack walking through. I never entered the gates but stood at the opening of the gates. Once standing at the gate the Lord allowed me to peer in.

What I saw was unexpected but confirmed the times and season that we are in. My eyes focused on white horses like I had never seen before. The images of these horses were so clear and the colors, the sheer whiteness of the horses was beyond the purest of white known on earth. The details of the muscular build and their manes where like silk, so smooth, with every hair in place.

As I marveled I saw people everywhere and their only job was to attend to these horses. Some were putting on bridles and others were taking take of the saddles. As I continued to gaze I began to try and count the horses yet the more I counted the more I saw making them without number. At this I was then brought back into the funeral home where the service was coming to a conclusion.

As I sat there overwhelmed by what I had just seen, I heard the Lord speak to me these words. HEAVEN IS GETTING READY TO RIDE!

Heaven's Riders! Vision of the Apostle John

Lets now peer into an account from Scripture where Heaven's armies are ready to ride.

Remember we are in the "year of the door." Heaven is now at your gates. The Apostle John was granted the extraordinary privilege of actually viewing a move of God from Heaven's perspective. Transported by the Spirit of God, He saw this end-time move from His very Throne.

From Revelation 19:11—

"And I saw heaven opened, and behold, a white horse,

and He who sat on it is called Faithful and True, and in righteousness He judges and wages war... And the armies which are in heaven, clothed in fine linen, white and clean, were following Him on white horses" (Rev. 19:11-14).

Heaven's armies are riding, following Jesus through an open heaven into the earth. What a picture of breakthrough! And what a picture of the midnight riders.

Note that Jesus judges and makes war. There's a key progression within this simple statement. God first renders judgment on a matter. He then makes war to establish His verdict in the earth. In other words, the verdict comes before the actual turnaround. We then become announcers and enforcers of Heaven's judgement.

I personally believe that the depiction of Revelation 19:11, of Jesus on His white horse judging and making war and coming with Heaven's armies, is directly correlated to Daniel 7:22, the Turnaround Verdict. It's the ultimate midnight hour. The saints are waging war against an antichrist spirit, and being overcome. But judgement is rendered in favor of the saints, and all of the sudden Heaven breaks in. The tide turns.

He judges and makes war.

Lets also note that somehow these horses and riders are able to bridge the dimensions to bring Heaven's authority, vitality and resources to bear upon our world. Friends, there's more to "rising up to meet the Bridegroom" than we may first perceive. The Lord is calling us to literally "come up higher" to perceive the activities of His Throne and movements in the earth. Hear the trumpet, and rise up to meet Him!

The Glory Revolution

Revelation 19:11-14 actually conveys a spiritual revolution which is catalyzed by a verdict from Heaven's Court. And in the spirit of Moses, or the Maccabees, or Paul Revere and his midnight ride, it's time now for a similar revolution which shifts the power base of nations from subjugation to freedom.

The context of this glory procession is powerful. Heaven opens. Jesus scend upon the Mount of Olives, Mount Zion and the 'here they dethrone an antichrist Pharaoh and reclaim et earth.

is in context with a wedding where He joins His covenant people to Himself.

That said, when the white horses of the Lord appear, know that heaven's movement is truly at hand. And we have the privilege of synergizing with Jesus and His new move!

Not only does the Bible culminate with a spiritual revolution, but the journey of God's people from slavery to freedom begins with a spiritual revolution. According to Exodus 12:12, God waged war against the gods of Egypt and the government of Egypt to begin a freedom movement during Moses' day. Passover. Deliverance from Pharaoh as the Red Sea parted. A covenant of marriage in the wilderness. And finally, the Promised Land.

This freedom movement set a precedent for the nations. And it provides a template for the "Moses Movement" prophesied for today. As we've mentioned previously, Bob Jones prophesied this movement will marry the miracles of Exodus with the miracles of Acts. Revolution and glory... as Cindy Jacobs described it, a glory revolution!

The Midnight Riders are Breakers in the Spirit

Some of the midnight riders are human. Some are angelic. It's so important to be in synergy with the angelic realm and the activities of God's Throne as we move into this next season. He wants us to move together to catalyze breakthrough.

First and foremost, the midnight riders, both human and angelic, are catalysts of breakthrough. They prepare the way of the Lord by enforcing His judgements in the earth. All barriers or resistance must yield to the breaker, and all enemies must succumb to this manifestation of Heaven's authority.

They simply have no choice.

The prophet Micah provides a great picture of what we've come to call "the breaker anointing." And his work has everything to do with the awakening and great procession which follows.

> I will surely assemble all of you, Jacob, I will surely
> gather the remnant of Israel. I will put them together
> like sheep in the fold; like a flock in the midst of
> its pasture they will be noisy with men.

> The breaker goes up before them; they break out, pass
> through the gate and go out by it. So their king goes on
> before them, and the Lord at their head" (Micah 2:12-13).

The breaker—the midnight rider—goes through the gate. And as the breaker goes out, the multitudes become released from captivity. They go out from their places of isolation and join in a great procession together.

I hope you see the parallels in the imagery between this scripture and the parable of the midnight cry. In fact, I hope it haunts you—in a holy way, of course. Because many of you are called as catalysts of God's turnaround. Breakers. Midnight riders sent by God to forge a new reality in the earth.

Best of all, the king goes before them, and the Lord at their head. This is a hidden facet of the Kingship anointing, and it enthrones Jesus in the earth. Not just figuratively, but one day even literally.

Angel of Breakthrough

Exodus becomes a prototype for us in this quest. The Lord rendered judgement in favor of His covenant people. Freedom was decreed. And a revolution ensued which was fought by God Himself. No nation on earth has ever experienced the execution of God's verdict of justice like Egypt. The Breaker broke open. And a captive people made their way to the Promised Land.

My friend Randy Demain "saw" this exodus once as part of an encounter with the Lord. And in the encounter, the Lord spoke of His angel as an angel of breakthrough. It really resonated. And it helped me see the story from a much different perspective. Exodus provides a picture of Heaven's breakers in action.

God sent an angel of breakthrough to lead Moses and his people out of Egypt. This angel escorted them through the wilderness and to the Promised Land. Note that this angel of breakthrough is distinct from other angels in God's created order. Scripture calls him "the Angel of the Lord." His name is capitalized—an honor conveyed through the typography of the original Hebrew.

And there's every reason to believe this honor is due. Because scripturally, the "Angel" referred to in these passages is most likely Holy Spirit. I want to be clear—Holy Spirit is the ultimate breaker! He is the essence of the breaker anointing.

After Moses died, this same Angel partnered with Joshua to cross over and begin possessing the Promised Land. The same breakthroughs ensued.

But after Joshua passed on, Israel fell into a downward spiral. They began to follow the way of the previous settlers, and worship other gods—the very sin the Angel of the Lord had warned against. Lets pick up the narrative here.

Judges 2 records an astounding prophetic directive delivered to all of Israel by the Angel of the Lord. To my knowledge it is the only time in the Bible where an angel of the Lord tangibly appears to audibly address an entire nation. It was essentially His "State of the Union Address."

Note that the Angel of the Lord is distinctive from other angels in God's created order. This honor is conveyed even through the typography of the original Hebrew. And there's every reason to believe this honor is due. Because scripturally, the "Angel" referred to in these passages can only be either Holy Spirit or the pre-incarnate Christ.

> Now the Angel of the Lord came up from Gilgal to Bochim.
> And he said, "I brought you up out of Egypt and led you
> into the land which I have sworn to your fathers; and I
> said, 'I will never break My covenant with you, and as
> for you, you shall make no covenant with the inhabitants

of this land; you shall tear down their altars.' But you have not obeyed Me; what is this you have done?

"Therefore I also said, 'I will not drive them out before you; but they will become as thorns in your sides and their gods will be a snare to you.'"

When the Angel of the Lord spoke these words to all the sons of Israel, the people lifted up their voices and wept. So they named that place Bochim; and there they sacrificed to the Lord" (Judges 2:1-5).

The name "Bochim" means weeping. The movement of the Angel of the Lord from Gilgal to Bochim conveys the journey of Israel from the time of circumcision, when God rolled away the reproach of Egypt, until his "state of the union" address after portions of the Promised Land were possessed and inhabited.

The Angel of the Lord appeared in order to bring the tribes of Israel into the next phase of possessing the land—what my friend Randy Demain calls the "second wave of breakthrough." But the Angel could no longer move with God's people because they had violated God's covenant... and even worshiped demonic powers.

The Angel vacated the premises. And the nation came to ruin.

When the spiritual guardianship of the land was rescinded, homeland security immediately failed. Borders suddenly became very porous. Foreigners, essentially terrorists, began to flood through these borders to plunder the nation. And the Jewish people became captives in their own Promised Land.

Not surprisingly, Judges 2 is actually a powerful warning to the United States of America and other nations as we move forward. Pride, especially open defiance of God, comes before a fall. Israel experienced the

> WHEN THE SPIRITUAL GUARDIANSHIP OF THE LAND WAS RESCINDED, HOMELAND SECURITY IMMEDIATELY FAILED... AND THE JEWISH PEOPLE BECAME CAPTIVES IN THEIR OWN PROMISED LAND. NOT SURPRISINGLY, JUDGES 2 IS ACTUALLY A POWERFUL WARNING TO US ALL. PRIDE, ESPECIALLY OPEN DEFIANCE OF GOD, COMES BEFORE A FALL

consequences of their defiance, and if we're not sincerely deliberate in our repentance and honoring of the Lord, America could experience this same measure of discipline.

I Will Send My Angel Before You

Though the address by this Angel was unprecedented, the people of Israel were actually very familiar with Him. Again it was this Angel who brought God's people out of bondage under Pharaoh's idolatrous dictatorship. He led them across the waters, through the desert and into the Promised Land. His introduction to Joshua compelled Israel's great general to fall on his face.

God even made a promise to the 12 tribes regarding the Angel. It's worth rehearsing so that you can see the full context of His final address to the people. From Exodus 23:

> Behold, I am going to send an angel before you to guard
> you along the way and to bring you into the place which
> I have prepared. Be on your guard before him and obey
> his voice; do not be rebellious toward him, for he will not
> pardon your transgression, since My name is in him.

But if you truly obey his voice and do all that I say, then I will be an enemy to your enemies and an adversary to your adversaries.

That's our God! I have long felt this passage is a sacred commissioning for the movements of our day. It is also a promise from the Lord to many of you reading these pages. Beginning now. May the word of the Lord leap off the page and into your spirit!

For many of you, it's turnaround time. Your personal journey is now becoming a glory procession. God is sending His angels before you to prepare the way, and to guard you and protect you and bring you to the place He has personally prepared for you.

Ok. Lets look at the next verse in the passage. This is where things get sobering.

> For My angel will go before you and bring you in to the land
> of the Amorites, the Hittites, the Perizzites, the Canaanites,

the Hivites and the Jebusites; and I will completely destroy
them. You shall not worship their gods, nor serve them,
nor do according to their deeds; but you shall utterly
overthrow them and break their sacred pillars in pieces...

God's original charge to the Israelites mandated they not succumb
to idolatry or erect pillars of idolatry in the Promised Land. As you can
see by the warning of the Angel of the Lord, they failed massively in
this. Yet over generations, He never changed His mind. He held them
to the same standard.

One of the greatest lies pushed on the body of Christ is that the
spirit of the age should dictate the standard by which mankind should
be evaluated. God's heart is true, and His commandments infallible.
Neither rock stars or rock star leaders have the right to redefine what
God determines to be sin.

Jesus Christ is not the same God as Allah or Buddha or the Queen
of Heaven or other gods worshiped in the religions of the world. He
stands alone. His life and blood, given on your behalf, prove this to be
true. And He alone is worthy and deserving of your devotion.

The Angel of the Lord and Gideon

After the Angel of the Lord vacated the
land, He did not show up again for an entire
generation. But eventually there was a re-
emergence. He was dispatched in response to
the sincere cries of God's people as they were
being overcome, marginalized, subjugated
and abused within their own covenant
boundaries.

UNTIL THIS COVENANT
RESTORATION THE
ANGEL OF THE LORD
WAS FORBIDDEN TO
EVEN MOVE THROUGH
THE LAND. BUT
GIDEON'S OBEDIENCE
OPENED THE WAY FOR
THE ANGEL OF THE
LORD TO DELIVER
ISRAEL AGAIN

The Angel of the Lord appeared to
Gideon with a signal in the night. Time for turnaround. This Angel
was dispatched to literally pick up right where he left off—restoring
homeland security and securing Israel's covenant boundaries. By the
way, in America this is exactly where we are right now. God is recruiting
His midnight riders, His Gideons, to partner with Him and complete

the turnaround that has been initially released. I cannot emphasize enough that the same God who is encouraging us is also evaluating us. Will we advance in Him or return to a cycle of idolatry which will mandate the Angel's departure?

"Then the Angel of the Lord came and sat under the oak that was in Ophrah, which belonged to Joash the Abiezrite as his son Gideon was beating out wheat in the wine press in order to save it from the Midianites. The Angel of the Lord appeared to him and said to him, "The Lord is with you, O valiant warrior... The Lord looked at him and said, "Go in this your strength and deliver Israel from the hand of Midian. Have I not sent you?"

What a commission. The same angel who partnered with Moses to rescue God's people from Egypt to the Promised Land, the same angel who partnered with Joshua to possess the land, was now inviting Gideon into the sacred partnership. And they together were about to re-possess the land.

Only one thing stood in the way. Turns out that Gideon's dad was one of the original settlers who completely disobeyed the Lord by building on his land an altar to Baal and Ashtoreh. The open defiance of Gideon's father in erecting his sacred pillar was a primary reason the Angel of the Lord vacated the land in the first place.

Not a coincidence the Lord's first assignment to Gideon was to tear this thing down. Fulfilling the original call given to the people of God to "break their sacred pillars in pieces," and opening the door for the Angel of the Lord to return and move in God's covenant land.

Lets put it another way. Gideon's obedience to "divorce Baal" and restore covenant with the Lord were mandated by God to satisfy the standards of Heaven's Court. On a personal level, he dealt with the generational idolatry in his bloodline. On a corporate level, the repudiation of his father's idolatry secured for Gideon the covenantal authority to deliver the entire nation.

Until this covenant restoration the Angel of the Lord was forbidden to even move through the land. But Gideon's obedience opened the way for the Angel of the Lord to deliver Israel again. The Angel of the Lord and Gideon, reporting for duty!

Further, Gideon's actions not only prepared him for military victory, they actually prepared his land for military victory. The land mourns when defiled by man's sin and disobedience. The ground itself rejoices when repentance brings cleansing, and the glory of God again moves upon it.

The perceptive will see the message of the Maccabees within this story. Separation and rededication can launch a new beginning.

Special Ops Mission—Light the Lamps!

Gideon soon overcame Israel's fiercest enemies with a small band of special ops warriors. In fact Gideon's example has become the prototype of many special ops communities today. Sometimes small teams of highly trained, highly competent warriors are more effective than mighty armies.

Gideon's warriors came to the battle line fully armed. With swords, of course. But also a vast arsenal of secret weapons only special ops warriors are capable of handling. Fiercest ever seen in the earth. They stop the enemy right in his tracks.

I'm talking about lamps, of course. Burning lamps.

And at midnight, a cry was heard. Gideon's warriors all became Lamplighters. They lit their lamps and held them high. And at the speed of light the enemy was supernaturally defeated. Further, a revolution was started, a freedom movement that restored the Promised Land to God's covenant people.

Lamplighters. Midnight cry. I hope you don't miss the parallel. Or the potential.

Redefining the Forerunner Calling

I hope you can see that Jesus is redefining the forerunner ministry in this hour. He's expanding our understanding. This is part of the preparation work for His midnight riders so they can prepare the way for His expressions in the earth. Breakthrough. Turnaround. Glory! A Moses movement.

'ide to resound a midnight cry. Remembering that the
.ltimately a summons to a wedding.

.r this, at this very moment Jesus is again drawing many
disciples to Himself for personal renewal with Him. I love the
picture portrayed by Luke:

"After these things the Lord appointed seventy others also, and sent
them two by two before His face into every city and place where He
Himself was about to go" (Luke 10:1).

Like Gideon in his day, or Samuel or John the Baptist in their day, the
body of Christ is again in a forerunning season) We are bridging a gap,
breaking the way for a new era of history. As catalysts of breakthrough,
Jesus is sending His forerunners into the cities He is about to visit. Many
will soon prophesy, cast out demons, heal the sick, reap the harvest,
and multiply the same miracles which defined His own ministry. We're
going to see so much of this in coming months and years.

But the first priority of Jesus' heart is to send us before His face.

"Send" is an apostolic word. In fact, Luke records the Greek
word "Apostello" to describe the work Jesus was accomplishing. He
commissioned apostles, and sent them apostolically two by two before
His face into the city.

There has been such an emphasis on the latter expression of this
apostolic or forerunner calling—being sent into the city. But the first
dimension of this "sending anointing" is to propel God's forerunners
before His face. Without this raw encounter of intimacy with Jesus
perpetually fueling us, the apostolic or forerunner ministry invariably
succumbs to power plays and a political spirit.

Perhaps that is why this message is sounding again in this hour.
Lets rediscover the face and heart of Jesus. Lets regain our first-love
devotion as our primary identity before Christ.

John the Baptist described himself as a "friend of the Bridegroom"
whose passion is to hear the Bridegroom's voice. This must remain the
overarching identity and passion of today's forerunners as well, as we
carry out his legacy today.

And from the days of Gideon to the days of Elijah and John the Baptist to our day, the forerunner call is ultimately to prepare God's people for His coming.

How is this done? First by restoring their covenant with Him. This includes leading people to Jesus, but as covered here it is even more vast. Friends, if you miss this, you miss the greatest purpose of God's midnight cry. And perhaps of the forerunner ministry. Because the door is wide open for nations as well as peoples to enter into covenant with Him. And we must keep in mind that Heaven's Court will not be satisfied in this process of covenant restoration until the divorcement from Baal—historic and present idolatry—is complete.

We must also carry our lamps with us. Bringing an anointing of holy conviction which releases correction and redemptive exposure to our world. For far too long we've been all thunder and no lightning. Where is the shining of gentle conviction which pierces hearts and makes known the need for Jesus to our world?

Here's a secret. As the glory returns, so the conviction returns.

So lets sum up what we've received so far. Below are ten characteristics which define or redefine the forerunner ministry in our time. If three or four or all resonate with you, you are probably being drawn into a deeper expression of this calling in your life.

1. *Bridegroom prophets*—cultivating a lifestyle of intimacy with God's heart, His voice, and His word. Core identity continually sourced in Christ's love. Loyal. Prophesying by God's Spirit the message of His covenant love. And mentoring God's people in covenant restoration!

2. *Kingship anointing*—set over nations and kingdoms. Growing in authority to governmentally rule in the spiritual realm and influence the earth. Elijah is a prototype. "No rain nor dew all these years except at my word."

3. *Throne Room Watchman*—as a "son of Issachar," receiving and responding to real-time prophetic revelation. Standing in God's

council, receiving divine intelligence, keeping watch.

4. *Pleading in His courts*—receiving real-time verdicts from Heaven's Court to release God's justice on earth as in Heaven. Jesus judges and makes war. We interact with Heaven's court and announce His judgements in the earth.

5. *The Breaker prepares the way*—intercession and even strategic level "special ops prayer" for breakthrough, for the restoration of God's glory, and ultimately even for the second coming of Christ. Preparing the heavens, bringing Heaven's alignment to earth.

6. *Preparing the bride*—restoring covenant where covenant has been breached. Being a guide or mentor. Developing community. Healing and bringing deliverance both personally and corporately.

7. *Signs and wonders*—your life testifies as an oracle from God, and your heart and hands demonstrate His miracles.

8. *Apostolic diplomacy*—influence and effective communication of prophecy and Kingdom solutions for leadership within the seven spheres of society which you are called by God to influence.

9. *Israel, the Jewish people, the nations*—standing for God's own covenant dream for His land and people to be fully established. Keeping always in mind that we are grafted into their covenant, not the other way around. We must be restored to our own roots!

10. *Lamplighters*—spiritual revolutionaries, midnight riders, announcing God's "now" word to awaken His covenant people and ignite the lamps of revelation, glory, covenant and prayer. Releasing an anointing of holy conviction which brings redemptive exposure. Like Moses, becoming a catalyst for spiritual revolution to shift nations into freedom—including, at times even regime change. He brings down rulers from their thrones!

As in Gideon's day, we have been confronting a m
we have received from God's own hand an extraordi
Just as Gideon's sacred pillar fell in his day the Washi
cracked in an earthquake in ours. A dramatic signal th
has been satisfied. Covenant with Christ has been res|

Now you and I and many others are being commissioned like Gideon to take back the land. As a forerunner you are part of Heaven's army as a catalyst of His freedom. Doesn't mean there won't be a battle. There was in Gideon's day, there was in Moses' day and there will be even in the days of the return of Christ.

But the Lord is with you, mighty man of valor. The Lord is with you, mighty woman of valor! His angelic breakers are being dispatched to work with you. You may even sense the tangible presence of the Lord and His hosts beside you as you read this. He is aligning you with Heaven's heart and movement. Nations will come to the brightness of your rising! In Jesus' Name!

Now—grab your burning lamps, mount your horse and lets roll. It's midnight. Time to launch an awakening! Heaven's riders are already at the gate.

CHAPTER NINE
A Glorious Procession

Hear the midnight cry. When the midnight riders are summoned, they ride to awaken the virgins and draw them to the Bridegroom. The bridal party lights their lamps. This leads to a glorious procession as they leave their places of comfort and isolation to meet the Bridegroom in the streets. Together they light up the night!

And they're headed to a wedding.

Virgins and lamps and midnight romance with the Bridegroom... Jesus' parable has all the nostalgic imagery of a classic Hallmark movie. But in reality it is so much more. The midnight cry is truly a summons to a wedding. But as we shared, it is also a summons to a revolution. An exodus.

Lets remember the Hanukkah Revolution. Covenant restoration is a primary way the bridal party will trim their lamps. Just as the Maccabees lit the lamp of their desecrated heritage, so lamps of covenant today are going to begin to blaze worldwide as cities and nations awaken, forsake their idolatry and realign covenantally with the Lord.

"Let My people go!" will be a primary expression of the midnight cry which will reverberate through these regions through the end of days.

And the angels of breakthrough will be really busy.

We are going to experience a foretaste of this power even in these next few years. Watch for great breakthroughs in freedom as this "burning lamp awakening" takes hold. "Nations will come to Your light, and kings to the brightness of Your rising!" (Isaiah 60:3)

Jesus is returning as a Bridegroom for His bride. But He is also coming with a vengeance that is currently unimaginable against an end-time Pharaoh who will have literally coerced the world into submitting to his idolatry and slavery. The midnight wedding is in context with a "Moses movement" against this form of global idolatry manifesting pure evil at its core.

Please understand. The same sentence of judgement against Pharaoh is the very summons God issues to His bridal party. And in both cases, an exodus is a result.

A great procession. A glorious procession. Let My people go!

The Glory Train

What does the fire on the lampstands represent? On a personal level it represents our passion, our hearts, our covenant, our worship.

But it was no coincidence the Lord lit our lamp at our wedding as we were singing, "Glory, glory, send Your glory!" Because the fire on the lamp ultimately represents the restoration of God's glory. And we are entering into this time of seeing His glory restored.

> And this is the vision I had. The train had come and I
> boarded it. I had a ticket and a seat. It was a very long
> train and it didn't have any boxcars on it. It was all just one
> long, large train and you could see from the beginning of
> the train to the end of it. There were literally thousands
> of people on this train and they were all sitting down.
>
> So I found my seat and I sat down too. And I was wondering
> where's this train going? What is this train? I saw the

Conductor come by so I asked Him, "What is this train?" He said, "This is the Glory Train!" Now I said, "Where are we heading?" He said, "To any city that wants it."—Bob Jones.

In 2009 Bob Jones received an extraordinary vision of the restoration of God's glory. He saw it coming like an unstoppable train—a Glory Train. According to Bob's word, the glory lifted due to the pride and idolatry of many carrying His presence and power through the mid 1970s. But the Lord gave him a solemn promise that he would live to see the beginning of this restoration move.

Bob Jones. His very name sounds like a railroad man. But he was one of the most prolific prophetic voices of the 20th century. Jolene and I were privileged to become friends with Bob and his amazing wife Bonnie a few years before he passed on. It turned out we were both working on the same tracks—seeing the restoration of God's glory—but from different ends of the line.

Bob of course, came from Heaven down. And through our efforts in repudiating idolatry and restoring covenant, we were coming from the ground up!

But Bob's vision portrays what I imagine this bridal awakening and procession is going to be like. I'll share a few more nuggets in a moment. But first let me tell you how Jolene and I were "grafted in" to Bob's vision.

It came while we were on vacation. We had just visited all 13 original colonies in 2014, in what we called the "Glory Procession." Traversing the geographic east gate of our nation, beckoning the glory of the Lord to be restored through this gate. It was during this time we went to Faneuil Hall to receive the "Turnaround Verdict."

After the tour we took a few days in Virginia Beach to recover. Jolene loves to set her chair up just close enough to the water that the waves touch but the sharks don't bite. Anyway, we sat our chairs in the wading water… and promptly fell asleep.

I was awakened by the roar of a fighter jet from an airbase nearby. And as I awoke, the Lord showed me a vision. I saw tracks being laid from Virginia Beach to San Diego. There was a locomotive engine rolling on the tracks which was silver and gold in color. The smokestack was unusual, because the steam coming from it looked more like a tornado. And the tornado stretched all the way up to the clouds.

At that moment I heard the phrase "Glory Train." And I knew the Lord was speaking about the restoration of His glory.

Whirlwinds often represent God's glory. Ezekiel saw a whirlwind as it departed the Temple after God's own people embraced idolatry. He also saw this whirlwind return to the Temple "by way of the gate facing east."

The disciples also perceived the glory of God as a whirlwind. After Christ's resurrection, they were praying in the upper room when they heard the sound of a mighty, rushing wind. And what looked like tongues of flaming fire rested on each one. They began to speak in other tongues, ignited by this flaming fire.

You're going to see this too.

It was this prophetic experience which led to the two Glory Train journeys we facilitated in 2016 and 2017. The first journey, as noted, was focused on national turnaround. We actually began on my birthday, March 4. I felt this was appropriate given that Isaiah 49 describes God as "marching forth as a warrior." We went to all 50 states, governmentally releasing God's Turnaround Verdict from Daniel 7:22. Phenomenal results followed which even affected the 2016 election. There are so many stories to tell about this that another book just might be appropriate.

Our second journey, also noted, began on August 18, 2017. I love Deuteronomy 8:18 because it promises the release of wealth to establish God's covenant. We felt to make another run across the nation, this time straight through from Virginia Beach to San Diego. Our public assignment was to governmentally declare the release of God's glory as a bridal canopy across the nation. As we shared in "The Midnight Turnaround," our private assignment was to receive communion and seek the Lord to expose the betrayer.

It was interesting how the Lord orchestrated our journey. We had to spend a couple of extra days in Washington DC because a special White House meeting had been postponed til that very time.

So quite literally, the White House became a stop on the Glory Train!

You already know the tremendous shifts which took place as we culminated the journey. With betrayal and abuse exposed from Hollywood to Washington at a level we had not yet seen in our time. This exposure and conviction is merely part of the purifying process which leads to the restoration of God's governmental glory.

And it's coming. Now.

Global Glory Revolution

Jolene and I were so glad to visit with colleagues at the Global Prophetic Summit in November 2017. Cindy shared with us personally that the Lord told her 2018 is all about the glory! And at the national roundtable, we discovered that prophet after prophet had also received a similar word. That's great news!

I want to emphasize again that the same man who prophesied the Glory Train also saw God's end-time movement as a marriage of the miracles of Exodus with the miracles of Acts. A global Glory Revolution!

Greatest Harvest of All Time

That said, here are a final few perceptions from Bob's word. The big capital letters are my way of emphasizing a few points you really need to take to heart:

> We're in a time of the coming glory. We're in a time of
> rain. I believe this rain is going to be literally like what
> they call a latter rain. I believe what's getting ready to
> take place really is the latter rain and it will never end. I
> also believe it is the reign of a King. I believe that WE'RE
> GOING TO BEGIN TO ANOINT JESUS AS KING...

> God loves the Church and I believe the enemy has walls around
> the Church that kept the Church imprisoned. The glory is
> going to blow those walls down and the Church is coming
> out to accomplish some things it was meant to do. AND THE

CHURCH WILL EXPERIENCE THE GREATEST HARVEST
OF ALL TIME THAT WILL NEVER COME TO AN END.

So we're on that glory train and any time you hear a train
whistle just say this in your thinking, "I'm on that train,
I'm on God's glory train! My future is in His glory train
and that's where I'll abide with Him! And all of my time
down here, that glory train will get bigger and bigger
because when it stops in the city, that city will no longer
belong to the enemy. It will belong to the Father."

GET READY FOR ENTIRE CITIES TO BE SAVED. And
get ready for the glory to shine at night like streaks of
flames; like fireworks to where you'll visibly begin to
see His glory. It's a coming glory but I don't believe we
have to wait long for it to come. I believe it's AT THE
DOOR WAITING and shortly it will come through...

Jon here. Now that's what I'm talking about. I can even hear the train
whistle as I write. Behold the Bridegroom. He's coming. Rise up to meet
Him!

Mission to the Virgins

Few things stir the human heart more than the prospect of a
midnight romance. There's something raw, almost seductive about it. If
the returning lover is actually a fierce warrior fighting for the freedom
of his bride, so much the better. Such nobility of purpose, of pursuit,
of unrelenting passion! It has the power to overcome the coldest heart.

And if you factor in that this frontlines warrior is actually a King...
well you might have just pushed the limits even of fairy tales. Because
some stories are just too good to be true.

But this one actually is. Like a special ops warrior returning for the
girl he betrothed, Jesus is returning for His bride. Meanwhile she has
forsaken all others, and is spending every hour of her redeemed life
preparing for this moment.

Here's another aspect which seems a little f
This midnight bride is identified as a virgin.

This aspect of Jesus' parable has been ver
Who are the virgins that Jesus is awakening?
Catholic church? Do they represent all believer
Or do the virgins refer solely to the nation of Is

I'm going to submit to you that the real me
profound than anything we have seen.

Restoring Virginity

One consistent commentary surrounding the parable of the ten virgins is that Jesus couldn't return in our day because there aren't enough virgins remaining in the world to actually make up a bridal party. I guess it's a joke. But I find it offensive.

Part of the salvation Jesus won for us is the reverse engineering of our virginity. We have all sinned and fallen short of the glory! It is only through Jesus' own body and blood that our virginity is genuinely granted, and our hearts and lives become pure in His sight. This salvation includes deliverance from present compromise as well as generational compromise that has been carried over in our bloodlines.

> COULD IT BE THAT THE VIRGINS REPRESENT CITIES, STATES, OR EVEN NATIONS WHO HAVE DIVORCED THEMSELVES FROM THEIR HISTORIC IDOLATRY, AND RESTORED COVENANT WITH GOD?

Note that this salvation must be worked out in each and every life. On a very personal level, sexuality forms bonds which join you to another person to the extent you biblically become one. Therefore to receive a new beginning it's important to cut the ties in the spirit, soul and body which have formed through your intimacy with others. Release to them what belongs to them, and call back to yourself what belongs to you. I would even suggest approaching Heaven's Court to receive mercy and a new beginning. And as part of your new beginning, ask the Lord to annul all covenants made between you and any other partner. Ask Him to sever all ties.

And above all, forgive. More bonds to others are held in place through than anybody realizes. Forgive and let go.

he way the Lord led Jolene through this restoration process. not just separate herself from her past. She also entered into enant with Jesus. Jolene was already saved, of course. But she gave herself to Him in a way she had never done before. Covenantally she gave over the reins of her life, her heart, her time, and allowed Jesus to become her all in all. It wasn't easy. But she devoted herself to Him.

And therefore it's no coincidence that seven years later He showed up at our wedding as He did. Lighting the fire of the unity candle in front of everyone, on the first day of Hanukkah, while we were singing "send Your glory!"

Jesus will do the same for you. His love language toward you will of course be unique. So will your journey. But as you devote yourself covenantally to Him, you will see His restoration flood every area of your life. He will make all things new! Including your virginity.

A primary key to virginity is loyalty. And for loyalty to be genuine, it must be tested. Note that when the virgins all awoke, they awoke alone. With no other lover sharing their beds.

New Womens Movement

Here's another point on the awakening of the virgins. Sometimes the most obvious revelation is so completely hidden that it's almost supernatural. But Jesus is prophesying something else through this parable of the wise and foolish virgins. He is coming to His handmaids. The virgins who awaken, arise and light their lamps also represent a new womens movement that will soon sweep the earth!

Jolene received a very strong dream on this early in the morning of April 21, 2017. She writes:

So I'm getting a full download from the Lord, which even in the dream I knew was amazing because I'm hearing from God at a clarity unlike any I have heard from Him before. It's like I knew the exact words, I knew the prophecy in advance, I knew what the Lord wanted to say, which is very unusual because typically He just gives me one word and I have to launch out and go. The only way that I can describe it is it was more than just words from the Lord. There was a weightiness and "chabad" or glory that was being given as well…

God is bringing a new womens' movement empowered by the prophetic and releasing His justice, especially to other women. What one carried, many will soon carry. God's justice is that they grow and mature into full stature in their identities and lives. The weight on their backs which mandated their sexuality be emphasized to gain favor and attention will be broken. Many who have been subject to sexual abuse and trafficking will be freed from this weight of bondage.

Many women with huge callings on their lives have had a huge weight on their backs as well. Before their life in Christ a primary thing that would bring them to the center of attention was their sexuality. And God is going to shift that. He is going to remove the heavy weight on their backs. And as the weight comes off and they stand in their full stature in Me, the attention will no longer be on their sexuality, it will be on their anointing!

Virgin Israel, Virgin Nations

The Apostle John perceived that the final end-time drama of Christ's return is actually triggered by the preparation of the bride in this regard. "Let us rejoice and be glad and give the glory to Him, For the marriage of the Lamb has come and His bride has MADE HERSELF READY!" (Revelation 19:7).

This is true for individuals, and it is also true for regions and even nations. As recorded in Isaiah 62, the prophetic statesman Isaiah prophesied that Jerusalem will no longer be termed forsaken or desolate. By inference, this means that Jerusalem had been forsaken and desolate—during a season of discipline from God's hand which was historically related to the embrace of idolatry.

The prophet calls Jerusalem "Hephzibah and Beulah. For the Lord delights in you, and to Him your land shall be married. And as a young man marries a virgin, so shall your sons marry you. And as a bridegroom rejoices over the bride, so shall your God rejoice over you!"

What does this mean? Here's a really important key. The desolate land becomes embraced again. And the Lord even references a restoration of virginity after she had defied God and defiled herself!

Isaiah begins this whole prophecy by declaring he won't stop praying until Jerusalem's salvation shines forth like a burning lamp.

You've read this book through, concentrating on every chapter. So you know already that fire is a sign of God's covenant, or His covenant restoration. Abraham saw a burning lamp when God cut covenant with Himself for the land and people Israel. Gideon conquered his enemies with a hillside full of burning lamps. The fire fell for David, for Solomon, for Elijah. The disciples in the upper room were consumed by fire.

And the Maccabees reconsecrated the Temple with a burning lamp after it had been defiled.

This gives incredible new meaning to the virgins who hear the midnight cry. They tend their lamps and go out to meet the bridegroom. Could it be that the virgins represent cities, states, or even nations who have divorced themselves from their historic idolatry, and restored covenant with God?

Could it be that in the end of days, God's virgin bride will be gathered from all the nations into a midnight procession, leading to a midnight wedding? Definitely something to ponder. Again the scripture prophesies to us:

> "Arise, shine; for your light has come, and the glory of the Lord
> has risen upon you. For behold, darkness will cover the earth
> and deep darkness the peoples; but the Lord will rise upon you
> and His glory will appear upon you. Nations will come to your
> light, and kings to the brightness of your rising!" (Isaiah 60:1-3).

Synergy of the Ages—with Dutch Sheets & Rick Curry

I want to close this chapter by sharing with you an amazing dream which sheds new light on the glorious procession of the bridal party. We are already fully engaged in this procession, as you will see. And so are our forefathers. Sojourning together to the very same tabernacle.

This dream was received by Rick Curry and highlighted Dutch

Sheets, who featured it in his book "Appeal to Heaven." It is used with Dutch's permission. Pay close attention to the procession described. Because in the dream, the procession led to a tabernacle. Just like the bridal procession.

One of the leaders in the dream is actually a representative of my Pilgrim forefathers. I have vowed before God to be such a witness for this nation. From the sixth chapter of "Appeal to Heaven" by Dutch Sheets:

In the dream, Rick found himself in an old wooden tabernacle, much like those found years ago on Christian campgrounds. It was dark inside and as he looked for lights, an elderly man approached, asking if he'd like a tour. Rick and I believe the "old man" represented Olam, the everlasting God and Ancient of Days.

The first thing this heavenly "tour guide" did was turn on all the lights and open all the windows, which were large pieces of hinged plywood, held open by poles. As the auditorium filled with light, Rick could see that it was huge, seating twenty-five to thirty thousand people.

The gentleman then escorted my friend to the platform and instructed him to sit on a stool. "Look out those windows," he said, pointing to the east. As Rick looked, he saw ships approaching in the distance. Those look like pilgrim ships, he thought. Sure enough, they were. Three thousand or more people from that generation of Americans disembarked, made a procession into the tabernacle, took their seats, and began worshipping God.

"Now, look out those windows," the man instructed, pointing in a different direction. As Rick looked, he saw pioneers coming in the distance—women in long skirts and bonnets, covered wagons pulled by oxen and other items depicting the era. Just as the pilgrims had, three to four thousand pioneers made a procession into the tabernacle while the previous generation stood and cheered: "Well done! Thank you for your hard work. Thanks for keeping the dream alive..."

When all the pioneers were inside, both generations began worshipping. After a few moments, the host approached again,

"Look out those other windows." Sure enough, another generation of Americans was approaching. "These are the planters," he said. "They built the roads, railroads, towns, and cities..."

This scene repeated itself with three more generations of Americans approaching and entering the tabernacle. Six generations in total were now present, twenty thousand or more strong, all worshipping. "The praise was so loud," Rick told me later, "the building was shaking."

At this point, the dream's host approached yet again, pointing to a seventh set of windows. As Rick watched, people from our era moved toward the building in cars and trucks. Just as the others, they made their entrance into the gathering—to great cheers, followed by passionate worship.

Seven generations of Americans now stood worshipping together, literally causing the building to vibrate from the sound of their praise.

After a few moments, the older man approached my friend yet again. "Watch these double doors," he instructed. As Rick looked, a representative from the pilgrims entered, walked up to the center of a bridge arching over the platform and began to prophesy God's plans and purposes for America. The people listened quietly as for several minutes he declared her corporate destiny, after which the worship ensued.

Five more times this was repeated—delegates from six generations decreeing and prophesying over America, each one followed by more worship.

Finally, when the time came for our generation to decree, the pattern changed. Approaching my friend with a very serious demeanor, the old man asked him a penetrating question, "Are you ready to take your place in the synergy of the ages?"

As you can imagine, hearing this phrase—that was first spoken to me in 2001—astonished me. Interrupting his account, I inquired, "Before the dream, had you ever heard this phrase? Have you heard me or anyone else ever mention the synergy of the ages?"

"Never," he assured me, as I stared at him in stunned silence.

This phrase, along with the fact that each generation of Americans was present, clearly pointed to the synergy created through multi-generational agreement. Seven generations; one nation. Many lives; one story. The fact that the phrase came in the context of a question is also significant: "Are you ready to take your place...?" It seems to me that God is asking an entire generation of American believers that question: "Will you join the appeal?" Each one will have to answer for her or himself. My prayer is that you take up the cause. We need you.

Continuing his account of the dream, Rick related his emphatic answer to the old man's question, "Yes, I'm ready to take my place."

"Go through the door and join the other leaders from your generation," he was told. Unlike the previous generations, ours had numerous representatives, many of whom he recognized. Together, they all marched into the room and took their seats. All of them, that is, except the last one in line. He, instead, headed toward the bridge.

"You were the last one, Dutch," he told me, causing the hair on the back of my neck to stand up! "You were the delegate from this generation. As you climbed the bridge, I noticed that unlike the other delegates, you were carrying something in your hands. When you reached the center, you began unfolding a white flag."

I was almost afraid to believe what might be coming. My mind was racing. Is he about to describe the flag that has just been given me—the Appeal to Heaven flag?...

"Upon reaching the center of the bridge, Dutch, you didn't begin prophesying and decreeing America's destiny, as the others had. Instead, you began waving the flag over the crowd in a figure eight, doing so for about ten minutes. As you did, the people were again passionately worshipping God."

This pattern is important. The number eight on its side—a figure eight—is the symbol of infinity or eternity. In ancient times, when a covenant was ratified by a blood sacrifice, the individuals entering into covenant would actually walk in a figure eight among the pieces of the sacrifice.

Why? They were swearing eternal allegiance to the covenant, just as we do in a wedding ceremony with our phrase "'til death do us part." Abraham probably did this when he and God "cut covenant" in Genesis 15.

By waving the evergreen in this "eternal" configuration, I was clearly emphasizing America's covenant with God. "We must honor the power of covenant," I was decreeing with my actions. "If we return to Him, He will war for us, defeating our giants." Also, by waving this flag, under which we were born, I was pointing us back to our roots as a nation—our birth, our purpose and our calling.

The dream is still alive, the flag was stating. Go find it. Revisit the stormy seas of the pilgrims, the dusty trails of the pioneers, or the bloody battlefields of Lexington and Concord. Read the sermons of Jonathan Edwards, George Whitefield, or John Wesley until the flame of the First Great Awakening burns in you. Read of Cane Ridge, the Second Great Awakening and Charles Finney until you burn with passion to see America become "the shining city on a hill" once again..."

(An Appeal To Heaven: What Would Happen If We Did It Again? pp. 57-64. By Dutch Sheets, Dutch Sheets Ministries, used with permission)

CHAPTER TEN
The Bridal Canopy

"Behold the Bridegroom. He's coming. Rise up to meet Him!" We began with a midnight crisis, a midnight watch. We saw how the Lord has decreed a midnight turnaround, releasing a midnight rider with a midnight cry. At the sound of this breakthrough cry the virgins will awaken and light their lamps in the midnight hour, and enter into a glory procession to meet the Bridegroom.

This great procession doesn't just begin sometime in the final hours of the end of days. It has already begun!

It's a glory revolution. Even now the Glory Train is rumbling through every city and town that welcomes it in. You might even hear the train whistle sounding in the distance. Soon it will be a roar. A midnight cry.

An anointing of holy conviction is already provoking multitudes to disengage from Jezebel's table and return to the Table of the Lord— the table of His covenant. They've awakened and resolved to join this great bridal procession.

All that said, where is the bridal procession ultimately going? Where does this glory train come into station?

Friends, you are actually invited to the ultimate destination wedding. Jerusalem. Jesus. Under a bridal canopy.

Since biblical days—in other words for thousands of years—the romance of a Jewish wedding has culminated under a small tent known as a "bridal canopy." The bridegroom and his bride would join hands and hearts under this canopy, with family and friends surrounding them. Establishing covenant for life!

Here's a fascinating detail. In former days, after the vows were exchanged, the new husband and wife would then roll the tent flaps down and actually consummate their marriage under the bridal canopy. I personally cannot imagine this. But a few of the guests served as legal witnesses that the covenant between the two had been sealed, and that the bride's virginity had remained intact until their moment had arrived.

It's no coincidence that, when God decided He wanted to dwell with His covenant people, He chose a tent to host His presence. The tabernacle is merely an expanded version of the chupah or bridal canopy.

According to Exodus 25 the Ark of the Covenant was to remain in the tent—an enduring witness of the marriage between the Eternal God and His people. The table of showbread, the table of the Lord, was to display His covenant meal. And within the folds of the tent, the lampstand or menorah was to remain lit perpetually. A burning witness to the covenant affection which God intended from the beginning to be a hallmark of His relationship with His people.

IN OUR RELATIONSHIP WITH THE LORD, WE OFTEN FOCUS ON OUR OWN NEED... BUT WE DON'T OFTEN PERCEIVE THE TENDERNESS OF HIS HEART OR HIS EARNEST DESIRE FOR OUR LOYALTY AND COMPANIONSHIP.

In our relationship with the Lord, we often focus on our own need for affirmation, for affection, for Him to know our hearts. But we don't often perceive the tenderness of His heart or His earnest desire for our loyalty and companionship. I've experienced many times with the Lord where His presence filled my heart, and we communed together without saying a word. I've also had times where His closeness was brought to an abrupt halt by my own insensitivity.

You know the feeling. In the midst of an intimate conversation, it is often very painful when your companion decides to interrupt the flow. Emotionally you simply withdrawal. I have found it's sometimes the same with God.

Beloved, don't break the flow. Sometimes your texts can wait. So can the call, the ballgame, the sale at the store, or any one of a million distractions. From a lover to the beloved, sometimes the highest worship, the greatest gift you can bestow, can simply be the gift of your undivided attention.

God never forgets those moments. And like you, He really wants more of them with you. Why not take some time at His table, under the tent. Give Him the gift both you and He treasure the most.

Tabernacles

I find it very poignant that as the midnight cry is heard and the bridal procession begins, the burning lamps of nations will gather in Jerusalem for this end-time marriage celebration. Probably around Mount Zion and the Temple Mount. The Lord called Israel and the nations to remembrance there, to gather in tents every year according to their tribe and celebrate the Feast of Tabernacles.

Of course, this is the same location where David first set up a tabernacle, a bridal canopy to host God's presence with 24-7 adoration celebrating Israel's King. After David sinned, it's where he repented. And then saw holy fire fall there, preserving Jerusalem and restoring his own heart.

It's the place where God commanded that the fire on the altar must never go out.

> FROM A LOVER TO THE BELOVED, SOMETIMES THE HIGHEST WORSHIP, THE GREATEST GIFT YOU CAN BESTOW, CAN SIMPLY BE THE GIFT OF YOUR UNDIVIDED ATTENTION. GOD NEVER FORGETS THOSE MOMENTS.

Solomon opened the Temple there and the glory of God fell in such a magnitude that His priests couldn't even stand to minister. The disciples gathered there in an upper room and the glory again swept in, baptizing them with the fire of the Holy Spirit.

God calls Zion His Throne. And His eyes will always be open, His ears attentive to the worship of His people on this mountain.

It's on this mountain that the spiritual revolutionaries known as Maccabees risked it all to take back their heritage. They lit the burnt out candles of the menorah to reconsecrate their Temple to the Lord.

This Hanukkah miracle became a prototype for the miracle God performed at our own wedding, in a storefront church some six thousand miles from Zion's hill. A summons had come to a faithful bride seven years beforehand, highlighting December 20. And when the Lord drew Jolene and me together, a mystery was revealed. Hanukkah marked the date this covenant bond was sealed. And God came with power. Lighting the unity candle of our menorah as all of our wedding guests watched and worshiped.

Remember it was on the anniversary of Hanukkah that God chose to descend in power and fill Miriam's womb. She conceived the Light of the World. As this Child grew into manhood, He too fell in love and decided to get married.

This relationship cost Him everything—not only His reputation but even His own body and blood. He died on a cross just outside the gates of Zion. Most thought God had abandoned His bride. As He drew His last breath, few understood that He was giving His life to redeem her.

Then God's power fell once more, this time to resurrect the Son of God, the Redeemer of Mankind. His bride awakened for the very first time. Like so many of her forefathers, she lit her lamp of love, of devotion and went out to meet Him. Joining as part of a glorious procession which culminates as all the nations gather under Zion's bridal canopy, for the wedding of the ages.

Because God remembers. And His burning lamps are coming home.

Rome to Jerusalem 2018

We're hoping to experience a foretaste of this end-time reunion in 2018, with a special prayer journey from Rome to Jerusalem culminating on the Feast of Tabernacles.

To understand its significance, lets briefly explore a piece of Jewish history surrounding the final menorah that was burning in the Temple when it was destroyed. This final Temple menorah, most likely relit by the Maccabees, was captured in Israel and carried off to Rome.

After the Maccabee revolt, the Roman empire overtook Greece and became the uniting force of global governance throughout the

Mediterranean region. Jesus was born under Roman rule. Unfortunately the years following Jesus' death and resurrection were marked by great despair for the Jewish people. In 70 AD Jerusalem again came under siege. Jews who were not taken captive escaped, and scattered over the face of the known world.

Rome destroyed the Second Jewish Temple during Tisha b'Av, the exact anniversary of the destruction of the first Jewish Temple. The Temple menorah was plundered from the Temple and carried to Rome on the backs of Jewish slaves. The freedom lamp had succumbed to captivity. The fire went out.

The Titus Door

Near the ancient forum, not far from Rome's Campidoglio or Capitol Hill, a giant victory arch was erected to honor Rome's global domination. The Arch of Titus famously features a sculpted panel depicting the scene of Jewish slaves carrying the Temple menorah into the city. Celebrating Rome's conquest of Jerusalem.

Remember 2018 is the year of the door. The Arch of Titus represents the doorway by which the Jews entered into all of Europe in shame, prejudice and subjugation. Their dignity was crushed. Their most precious and sacred treasures were plundered.

The culture of the day, syncretized with Christianity, mentored the entire western world in hating the Jews. Pogroms and expulsions ran through the centuries, in all nations and most emerging expressions of Christianity. Ultimately this prejudice became embodied in a man and movement that systematically exterminated more than 6 million men, women and children during the holocaust.

We must do our small part, as empowered by Holy Spirit, in seeing the full reversal of this bondage.

The Roman Lampstand

Two centuries after the menorah was ripped from the Temple and handed to Rome, the Emperor Constantine sought for Rome to replace Jerusalem as the epicenter of religion. Symbolically, as the global lampstand for Christianity.

Over time, Constantine and his followers radically redefined the doctrines of Christianity. They divorced the faith of our fathers from our Jewish roots—including our Hebraic understanding of times, seasons and law.

And they hastily married Christianity to Roman beliefs and traditions. Temples became churches. The vestal virgins of Roman paganism became nuns. And as mentioned before, Constantine merged two pagan winter holidays with gospel accounts of Christ's birth to create the winter celebration we now call Christmas.

And whereas early church leaders shunned the worship of other gods, the hybrid created by this shotgun wedding proved much more tolerant. Syncretism. Many gods simply got an extreme makeover, gaining new identities as saints.

With all this said, Jolene and I love Rome. We were surprised and delighted to sense the pure presence of Holy Spirit over the region. God is moving powerfully in the city! And it is an honor to stand for God to release His full blessing and destiny for this ancient root of the Christian faith.

And without a doubt, so much good has come from this ground. The Reformation launched by Luther is seemingly more alive in the Catholic church now than much of the Protestant world. Salvation by faith in Christ alone is now an undisputed doctrine. Curial eyes are now often much more discerning regarding idolatry than their peers in other spheres of Christendom. Catholics today lead the pack in the pro-life movement, true heroes championing the unborn.

And sincere repentance to the Jewish people over the brutal legacy of anti-Semitism has brought tremendous healing.

Restoring the Lampstand to Jerusalem

While in Rome recently, I believe the Lord showed Jolene and me that it is now time to apostolically reverse this journey of the menorah. He desires to restore the burning lamp this year from Rome to Jerusalem.

Though there's a lot of speculation, nobody but God knows where the original Temple menorah actually is. But I believe the Lord desires for many of His leaders and intercessors to carry their own menorahs as a symbolic act of this restoration.

Like the bridal party that awakens at midnight, we are going to light our lamps and make a journey. This journey is going to culminate with Israel's Bridegroom, in a great celebration under a bridal canopy in the city He eternally calls home.

Jerusalem. 2018. The Feast of Tabernacles.

Like the branches of a menorah, the lampstand of our faith branches out to all the world. But it must be centered in Jerusalem, not Rome. We are grafted into God's covenant with the land and people Israel, not the other way around. By this journey we are apostolically conveying that Jerusalem must be honored as the geographic epicenter of both the Jewish faith and the Christian faith, because God identifies Zion alone as His geographic throne.

We are declaring the restoration in Jesus—Yeshua—of our Jewish roots. Of our covenant roots.

What's in this for Rome? Everything. Seeking God for this prophetic restoration by no means robs Rome, it frees Rome. By honoring God's original intention for His lampstand in Jerusalem, the lampstand of the Lord which genuinely belongs to Rome in Christ will immediately become greatly empowered.

That's the great power of God's restoration. And I sense prophetically you will see great renewal in Rome as a result.

The burning lamp belongs in His tent! What a picture of a move of God's Spirit in 2018 to reunite the burning lamps with the bridal canopy of His tabernacles movement. What an honor it will be to celebrate the Feast of Tabernacles in Jerusalem.

So friends, lets light our lamps—and from Rome to Jerusalem, lets go out to meet the Bridegroom in 2018. He's standing at the gates even now, waiting for our arrival. Not by might nor by power but by My Spirit, says the Lord of hosts!

Bridal Canopy—Prophetic Word for 2018 and Beyond

As we've mentioned, two feasts are being highlighted by the Holy

Spirit to us for the time span from 2018-2020. Hanukkah, or the Festival of Lights, when Jesus was most likely conceived. And the Feast of Tabernacles, when Jesus was most likely born. They represent a life cycle, a time of conceiving and birthing His plans for your future.

At the beginning of the book we shared many treasures about Hanukkah which I hope provide a frame of reference for you to perceive God's work today. I pray these revelations will do likewise.

At the 2016 Global Spheres gathering, Chuck Pierce and Robert Heidler gave a teaching about the Hebrew meaning of the coming year 5776. They prophesied that 5776 and 2016 would be remembered as the year of the "vav."

Vav is the Hebrew word-picture for the number six. And as Chuck and Robert both pointed out, vav looks exactly like a tent peg or a railroad tie. Neither had any idea we were planning a 50 state tour by train. But they began to prophesy about 5776-2016 as a year of connecting. Of driving your stake in the ground and even connecting the railroad tracks that have been disconnected! It was incredible confirmation as we planned the final phase of the tour.

Less than a year later, the Lord began to speak to me about 2017 through the symbolism of the Hebrew numbers. In August 2016, Jolene and I were participating in a reunion of Christian leaders who had taken a special class at Yad Vashem, the Israel holocaust museum, when He began to give very clear revelation.

Biblically, the number seven or "zayin" is a primary symbol of covenant. Which made 5777 of the utmost importance. It is actually formed by taking a "vav" and adding a crown! Immediately when I saw this, I sensed the Lord clearly speaking to my spirit, "For 5777-2017 I am going to crown the vav. Where My people have staked their claim in my promise, I am crowning their covenant commitment with My glory and My government!

Keep in mind that we were still approaching both the 2016 elections and the final leg of our Glory Train tour when I received this word from the Lord. We had literally staked our claim state by state to the turnaround God wanted to bring our nation. The word soon proved more accurate than I could have imagined.

The revelation the Lord gave for these two years is really important for you to understand what God is saying for 5778 or 2018. Because the number eight prophesies into the bridal canopy we perceive the Lord is granting. The Hebrew word-picture for eight, "chet," actually symbolizes both a door and a bridal canopy.

The graphic design of chet is unique, made up of two pillars connected at the top to form this door or bridal canopy. The pillars are made by a "vav" or six on the right side and a "zayin" or seven on the left.

Six and seven. That caught my attention because, well, I was born in 1967! And historically in that same year, Jerusalem was restored to Israeli sovereignty after the Six Day War.

Six and seven. God is taking the best of 2016 and 2017 and joining them together to release us into 2018. Further, the year 5778-2018 is forming a doorway into God's tabernacle or bridal canopy. As in David's day when He restored the Ark of the Covenant and then pitched a tent for God's glory, He is now establishing thrones of glory nationwide. A new tabernacles movement!

> GOD IS TAKING THE BEST OF 2016 AND 2017 AND JOINING THEM TOGETHER. FURTHER, THE YEAR 5778-2018 IS FORMING A DOORWAY INTO GOD'S TABERNACLE OR BRIDAL CANOPY

An awesome confirmation of this came when my friend David Bradshaw decided to host a 50 state, 50 tent gathering on the National Mall—over the Feast of Tabernacles—just as we began the Hebrew year 5778.

You can't make this stuff up, I'm telling you.

For this reason, we actually culminated our second Glory Train journey on the first night of Tabernacles in San Diego, returning to Washington DC just in time for the tent gathering after declaring the release of His glory coast to coast as a bridal canopy.

Okay, you missed it. The Glory Train or glory procession of this end-times bridal party culminates in the Tabernacle. We're forerunning this now. And it's the start of something really big.

Bridal Canopy—Three Experiences on the Glory Train

Let me read you in on a back story to all this which is pretty amazing. Back in 1996, Cindy Jacobs saw a vision of an "X" pegged into the four corners of America. The "X" represented the enemy's plan to "X out" or abort our nation's destiny. Glory departed. Cindy took counsel with Dutch Sheets over the vision. And as Dutch prayed into it, he saw a vision as well. It was like one vision answered the other.

Dutch saw this giant "X" transformed into a bridal canopy over the entirety of our nation. He saw the center pole pegged into the geographic center of our nation, and the tent itself pegged into all four corners. A bridal canopy of God's glory.

It was with this combined vision that Cindy Jacobs launched the 50 state Spiritual Warfare Network, the genesis of many prayer networks afterwards, including the Reformation Prayer Network which she now leads, and the Heartland Apostolic Prayer Network led by Dr. John Benefiel. We collaborate with both of them. And our Lamplighter family nationwide has devoted themselves to intercession towards this end too.

During the meeting launching the Spiritual Warfare Network, I was asked to take part in a prophetic action. We circled the room, representing the turnaround God was going to bring to transform this "X" into a bridal canopy. I then participated in a "wedding" under a Jewish prayer shawl often symbolizing a bridal canopy. Prophetically declaring the restoration of our national covenant, the marriage of America back to her God.

Since that time, the Lord has orchestrated my steps to prophetically walk through the different phases of this very work. Including divorcing Baal and seeing covenant with Christ nationally restored as a means to catalyze turnaround and prepare the way for the restoration of God's governmental glory. Both Glory Train journeys, but especially the second, were focused towards this end. Our primary focus was seeing His bridal canopy established coast to coast.

Accompanied by HAPN leaders Sandy Newman and DeeAnn Ward, we even journeyed to the geographic center of our nation—in

Kansas—to bear witness to God's great restoration.

And would you believe the monument there, commemorating this place as the geographic center of the Continental United States, is actually pictured like the Hebrew number "Chet." Eight. Two pillars connected up top to form a door or a bridal canopy.

You cannot make this stuff up.

Another prophetic experience came during the Glory Train journey just before venturing to Kansas to pray. The Lord began to speak to us about His bridal canopy related to situations then at hand. We were in St. Louis when I had the following vision. From our posting on September 11, 2017:

As part of our Glory Train journey, Jolene and I had the privilege of ministering at Life Gate International in St. Louis with pastors Kingsley and Glenda Walker… In the midst of the service the Lord gave me a download that I believe is extremely pertinent for today.

I had just prophesied about how an Amos 9:11 "Tabernacles Movement," restoring the fallen tabernacle of David, has now begun. I personally believe that the first global trumpet call came from Heaven amidst the rubble and ruin of September 11. The second global trumpet call for this restoration movement has come in this season.

Then I saw a vision. Two hurricanes—in Florida and Houston—were pictured on two big screens of a weather forecast, one on the left side and one on the right. I saw "Category 4" overlaid over both in bold block text.

Suddenly the "4" of each hurricane floated off of each screen over each hurricane and joined in the center area. They came together to form "4:4." This was amazing to me, as I had just ministered on Isaiah 4:4. Here's the text of this verse.

"When the Lord has washed away the filth of the daughters of Zion and purged the bloodshed of Jerusalem from her midst, by the spirit of judgment and the spirit of burning, then the Lord will create over the whole area of Mount Zion and over her assemblies a cloud by day, even smoke, and the brightness of a flaming fire by night; for over all THE GLORY WILL BE A BRIDAL CANOPY" (Isaiah 4:4-5).

Look at our floods. Look at our wild fires. I suddenly realized that, through natural disasters, America has been experiencing both the "washing" and the "burning." Both together are a sign to us. And both are a call to renewed repentance.

One final story about the Glory Train, and I'll be brief. You already know how, the moment we completed the coast to coast journey by pulling into California, a major shift occurred in Hollywood. Hugh Hefner died. He was the man largely responsible for the sexual revolution, taking covenant-breaking, misogyny, sex abuse to a whole new level.

At the very same time, all air traffic nationally and even internationally was suddenly grounded. Isn't that strange! We found this out during a meeting with Arthur Burk, who commented that it was possibly the greatest disruption in human transportation seen since the days of Noah.

Of course I inquired of the Lord. Why? I know this is subjective, but this was my immediate sense. God literally cleared the airways for His Bridal Canopy to be lifted up over the nation.

You cannot make this stuff up.

It's a sign to us. Because as we shift into 5778, the Lord is intent on establishing His bridal canopy over us. Personally, regionally, even nationally we are now entering into a "tabernacles movement!" His glory is being restored. And we are being given the opportunity to become thrones of glory to our Father's house...

We are on the Glory Train journey because we firmly believe that His glory is being restored to our land. Last year as we circled the nation on the tour, we knew we were presenting the Lord Jesus Christ with a wedding ring. America married to Jesus!

Through this tour we saw the Lord establishing His glory as a bridal canopy. Culminating 21 years of dedicated intercession. This covering is the redemptive potential we see for our land. A tabernacles movement. I believe our Glory Train journey is bearing witness to this, and I believe Awaken the Dawn is a sign of this as well.

But here's something you don't want to miss. Because ultimately the restoration of God's glory as a bridal canopy is for a wedding. State by state, America married to Jesus. Which is why our Revolution 2017 gathering has carried this focus. At a place called by God as "America's Ark of the Covenant," the Museum of the Bible.

Over Hanukkah. Our 14th anniversary. You simply cannot make this stuff up.

Lighting a Global Lampstand—Prayer Storm

The Lord has brought America through a midnight hour. We were nearly "Xed out." But His covenant has prevailed, and His bridal canopy will prevail. But we are not unique. Jesus deeply desires to bring nations through the sacred process of covenant renewal and the restoration of His glory.

A decade ago James Goll was roused from sleep by the audible voice of the Lord. And much like the prophet Zechariah, in this midnight cry the Lord spoke to him about a burning lamp. "I commission you to restore and release the global Moravian lampstand!" God resounded to the prophet.

Amber letters then appeared before James, forming the words "Prayer Storm." A global, 24-7 expression of worship and prayer.

On 12-12, 2015, during the Jewish festival of Hanukkah, James Goll imparted his mantle to Jolene and me for the global movement he birthed called "Prayer Storm." The transference of this mantle was humbling—a total surprise. A holy fire was imparted.

In the spirit of Judah Maccabee, Jolene and I felt to light the lamp and reconsecrate Prayer Storm from Jerusalem. I guess Jesus wanted us to return to the land of His birth for the birthing of this next phase. We departed on September 11, and landed in Israel on September 12, 2016.

Jolene and I prayed in Jerusalem, overlooking Mount Zion, to consecrate ourselves and this Global Prayer Storm movement. The next day the Lord unexpectedly responded to our consecration by meeting us at a little village called Shiloh.

Shiloh has quite a history. This was the original resting place for the Tent of Meeting, the Tabernacle, in the Promised Land. The Ark of the Covenant rested there for 369 years, from the reign of Joshua all the way to the days of the prophet Samuel. God's glory hovered over the Tabernacle, connecting Heaven and earth to the extent that Shiloh became the governmental center of Israel. The twelve tribes gathered at the Tent of Meeting to encounter the Lord and then possess their land.

In short, Shiloh became Israel's first "throne of glory." That is, until a corrupted priesthood provoked the Lord to lift His glory. Covenant with God was breached, and eventually the prophet Samuel sent the Ark of the Covenant into captivity.

Ichabod—glory departed—was declared.

The Ark of the Covenant never returned to Shiloh. When David restored the Ark, he built a tabernacle on Mt. Zion, Jerusalem for His resting place. Eventually the corruption of the priests and people, through idolatry and sin, caused the glory to lift from Zion as well.

Shiloh Encounter—Restoring God's Glory

Surrounded by the rocky ground and mountain vineyards of Samaria, I saw prophetically that the bridal canopy is returning. God is now restoring His glory to Shiloh. It was as though the blustery winds carried a verdict from Heaven's Throne. Ichabod erased. Glory restored.

This came so clear to both Jolene me. Of course, He is restoring His glory to Jerusalem as well. And to many cities throughout the earth where His glory once dwelt. That was really the point. If He could do this for Shiloh, He could do it for the nations. And I knew it was from this ground that the Lord wanted to commission the next phase of this Global Prayer Storm to restore the fire of His covenant and glory to Israel and the nations.

God wants to reset His lampstands and relight the flames. He wants to restore the burning lamps of first-love devotion to houses of prayer and Christian communities globally. I even sensed the Lord speaking about the restoration of His glory to the Jewish people, in a movement He called "Davidic Judaism." This might be above my pay grade. But I'm prophesying it!

Uncorrupted Priesthood Restoring the Ark

Another resonance from this sacred ground soon burst forth. Jolene just kept pacing and praying, which is uncharacteristic for her. As I looked a little closer, I saw she was wiping away tears. Because as with the prophet Samuel, the Lord had spoken to her, "It's going to take an uncorrupted priesthood to restore the Ark of the Covenant into the cities of the world."

Through many tears we both dedicated ourselves to stand before Him as priests of the Lord like Samuel. Daring to live uncorrupted for His glory instead of embracing the idolatry and corruption that causes His glory to lift. We are searching the nations of the earth for people of like, precious faith.

Like you. Willing to dedicate yourselves to be an uncorrupted priesthood before His Throne, qualified by Heaven for a move of His Spirit to be initiated.

Tabernacle of David—New Phase of Restoration

The encounter at Shiloh was very deep and totally unexpected. Looking over the hills, Amos 9:11 soon began to reverberate within my being. I knew it was somehow a seal of this new depth of personal consecration, and the rededication of the Global Prayer Storm movement.

If you're like me, you have this passage on the restoration of the Tabernacle of David memorized—backwards, forwards and sideways. It's God's promise of a global prayer movement centered on intimacy with Him, after the pattern of King David.

But if you're like me, you may not have read much beyond the initial promise of Amos 9:11. What is in God's heart as He restores this movement to the earth? Lets reach a little further.

> 11 "In that day I will raise up the fallen Tabernacle
> of David, and wall up its breaches; I will also raise
> up its ruins and rebuild it as in the days of old;

> 12 "That they may possess the remnant of
> Edom, and all the nations who are called by My
> name, declares the Lord who does this.

13 "Behold, days are coming," declares the Lord,"When
the plowman will overtake the reaper and the treader
of grapes him who sows seed; when the mountains will
drip sweet wine and all the hills will be dissolved.

14 "Also I will restore the captivity of My people
Israel, and they will rebuild the ruined cities and live
in them; They will also plant vineyards and drink
their wine, and make gardens and eat their fruit.

15 "I will also plant them on their land, and they
will not again be rooted out from their land which
I have given them," says the Lord your God.

Three things stood out to me. First, the Lord is restoring this
movement not only to bring us into a new level of intimacy, but also to
possess the nations which are called by His name. When we dedicated
ourselves at Shiloh for His global movement, my insides began to
quake. It was as if the very ground where Joshua launched his troops
to possess the land began to burst forth with anointing. An anointing
to possess the nations called by His Name!

Second point. Amos 9:13 actually prophesies that the mountains of
Samaria will drip with sweet wine. The mountains surrounding Shiloh
are right now covered with vineyards, for the first time in thousands of
years. In fact, we learned that Shiloh's wines are winning international
awards!

The mountains are dripping with sweet wine. An astonishing
prophetic sign that this movement which restores God's glory to cities
and nations is now at hand.

Third point. God promises His covenant people that He is planting
them in their own land, and they will never again be rooted out.

Note that this is in context with the end-time promise given regarding
the restoration of the Tabernacle of David. If you believe that this global
movement of worship and prayer is now being restored, if you see the

vineyards and validate the prophetic promise is now being fulfilled exactly as described, then you must also believe that the Jewish people now planted in the land must never be rooted out of their land.

I believe the Lord is reaching down from Heaven to synchronize us all with the end-time movement He is now bringing to birth. Amos 9:11 through 9:15. A Tabernacles movement. Take time now to dedicate yourself afresh to Him as an uncorrupted priest for this new move. Let Him realign you and synchronize you with His Throne. With the heartbeat of His timing and movement in your life. With your destiny.

The Lion Shakes His Mane

After we returned from Shiloh to Jerusalem, the Lord gave a defining vision to Jolene. She saw the raw power of the Lord's communion with His covenant people as they moved together in worship and prayer.

It's my honor to close our "Midnight Cry" with this vision of Jesus and His bride.

The encounter came as Jolene and I responded to a gracious invitation by Steve and Taffy Carpenter for a visit to their home. A little worship and prayer with friends, they suggested. We had no idea what we were getting into.

Steve and Taffy lead a ministry focused on Isaiah 19—pioneering the fulfillment of prophecy, a highway of worship to the Lord from Egypt to Israel to Iraq and beyond. Steve, Taffy and their kids began to lead us all in prophetic worship. Jolene had a visionary experience almost from the start. For more than half an hour!

Never has this happened before. But it was like she saw in the Spirit the flow of worship and prayer in the room, and how God is moved in turn.

Jolene's vision is redefining how we see the Lord. We pray it will be a gateway for your new discoveries as well. In her words:

I saw dancers, like ballerinas or modern dancers, swirling around the room with banners and flags, freely moving. Then I saw the Lion of the tribe of Judah sitting in the middle of the room. They would wave their banners over Him. And His mane would become the color of the banners they were waving. His mane would become the color of whatever they were dancing.

And then the Lion of the Tribe of Judah would shake His mane according to what we were praying in the room! He was roaring and shaking His head. Colors would then disperse everywhere. Releasing the answers from His Throne in concert with the movement of our prayers.

The first color was a light purple, which I took to be a priesthood color. I had been praying in the room for an unpolluted priesthood to come forward. Carrying over from a deep time of prayer in Shiloh, where the Lord strongly touched my heart with this desire. He raised up the prophet Samuel there. At the same time, a corrupted priesthood resulted in the Ark of the Covenant being sent into captivity.

As I prayed for this uncorrupted priesthood to arise, I saw this royal, light purple color flood the mane of the Lion of Judah. He would then roar, and shake His mane. And rays of purple would fly out from His mane!

The flow of worship and intercession in the room then kind of switched. From Jerusalem, we began to pray together for the east coast of the United States. That's when the dancers' banners changed to red. And the mane of the Lion changed to red, painted the color of red. And as the Lion roared and shook His mane I saw drops of His own blood raining down across the entire East Coast. His redemption will be seen!

Then the dancers' veils turned to a deep purple color. And I knew that this color represented the hills dripping with sweet wine. And then I was praying on the scripture in Amos 9 where the hills were dripping with sweet wine. So the Lion shook His mane again, and that propelled this new wine to the earth, spreading everywhere across the body of Christ!

I inquired of the Lord what the dancers actually meant, and He told me it was the intercession. The dancers symbolized our worship and intercession. And these whirling dancers activated the Lion of the Tribe of Judah, His roar and the shaking of His mane in real-time. The shaking of His mane brought the unstoppable propulsion of His answers to the earth!

Looking back at this vision, there are three themes of prayer that God is intensively responding to right now. The Lion of Judah is roaring! He is commanding an unpolluted priesthood to come forth.

Second—the blood of His covenant is being applied across the east coast and to America. Note that this vision occurred exactly a year before our second Glory Train journey, where we were assigned to receive communion and release the bread to expose the betrayer.

Third—the Lord is commanding for the 'new wine' to come forward all across the globe. A sovereign move of Holy Spirit. Note that Jesus saved the best wine of WEDDING FEAST… for the very last.

Beloved, Jesus has this wedding all planned out. And the midnight cry remains your invitation.

Behold the Bridegroom. He's coming. Rise up to meet Him!

Your Notes

Your Notes

Your Notes

LAMPLIGHTERS

About Jon & Jolene

Jon and Jolene Hamill love to share His heart and word nationally and internationally through ministry and media. Founders of Lamplighter Ministries and Directors of Burning Lamp Media and the Global Prayer Storm movement, they reside in Washington, DC.

Jon and Jolene are popular speakers in conferences and churches throughout America. In 2016 they led a prayer and revival journey called the Glory Train, touching all 50 states with God's promise for national turnaround. They have also taught and shared prophetically in Israel, Canada, Germany and Sierra Leone.

Jon and Jolene are the authors of the recently-published book "Crown and Throne: A Field Guide to Spiritual Revolution." In addition, they have authored numerous prophetic teachings which have appeared on the Elijah List, in Charisma Magazine and other publications. They share postings regularly through email, and host a weekly conference call which you are welcome to join. To connect with Jon and Jolene, please find us on the web at:

www.jonandjolene.us | www.lamplighterministries.net
www.prayerstorm.com
Email: admin@lamplighterministries.net

Made in the USA
Middletown, DE
16 June 2018